Margo's Memoirs

by

Marguerite Tarr-Boyington

RoseDog Books
PITTSBURGH, PENNSYLVANIA 15238

RoseDog Books
585 Alpha Drive
Suite 103
Pittsburgh, PA 15238
Visit our website at *www.rosedogbookstore.com*

ISBN: 979-8-88683-515-1
eISBN: 979-8-88683-603-5

Margo's Memoirs dedicated to my children:

- Caroline Tarr-Brown
- William L.Tarr, Jr.
- Dr. Julie C. Tarr

Margo Tarr Boyington

FASHION SHOWS: Coordinated fashion shows and commentaries, including two on television.

PAGEANTS: Coordinated Miss Rochester Pageant for two years – the entire production and had two finalists in the Miss America Pageant, Atlantic City, New Jersey. Judged Junior Miss American Pageants and other local pageants throughout New York State.

TV: Television commercials for shopping malls, Rochester, New York. Co-chaired the Rochester Miss America Pageant and conducted interview for New York State pageants.

RADIO: Recorded some programs for the Department of Education, Ottawa, Canada in French.

MAKEUP: Worked briefly for Zsa Zsa Gabor Cosmetics, Rochester, New York, doing makeup demonstrations. Also did makeup demonstrations for TV personalities in Rochester, New York.

FUNDRAISING EVENTS:

- Sister Cities International
- Federated Women's Club of Clearwater, Florida
- Arthritis Foundation
- Heimlich Foundation

Real Estate Background

- Twenty plus years in the real estate industry
- Cincinnati Board of Realtors – Director of Public Relations
- SRS (Senior Real Estate Specialist)
- Chelsea Moore Commercial Realtors - Marketing Director
- Realtor/Sibcy Cline Realtors. Ohio & Kentucky - 12 years
- Prudential Realty, Florida

Boards of Directors

- Cincinnati Editors Assoc.
- Ohio and Kentucky Chambers of Commerce
- Former member Public Relations Society of America
- Lookout Farms Homeowners Assoc. Kentucky
- Governors Point Homeowners Assoc. Kentucky
- President Gifu, Japan Sister Cities Assoc. Cincinnati, Ohio
- Chairperson Canadian Sister Cites Assoc. Cincinnati, Ohio

Education

- Thomas Moore College - Real Estate
- Rochester Institute of Technology - Photography
- University of Cincinnati – Journalism
- Speaks and writes French Fluently

Margo's Memoirs

This is my life ...

Where do I start

When did life drastically change?

Death of my father.

The early morning silence of May was shattered by the eerie sound of a collision between the final street car route and my father's new red Ford.

My father Fred, a handsome thirty-nine-year old engineer, was returning home from the most successful fishing trip of his life with his three favorite buddies. Several species of fish, including a ten-pound bass, had been thrown in an old tub. The smell would have been overwhelming to anyone else, but to him, it was a high. This huge bass was like a trophy.

Slightly intoxicated he drove his friends to their homes. Needing a cigarette, he reached down to the floor for his crushed pack of Camels, too late to see the electric streetcar headed in his direction.

What the hell is this...going the wrong way? he thought as his sentence ended in a scream; his car swerved, hitting a large oak tree in someone's front yard. Bleeding profusely he passed out.

A few neighbors awakened by the crashing sound rushed to the scene.

"Looks like he's still alive," one said, trying to move the steering wheel that was embedded in his chest.

"I'm calling an ambulance," said the somewhat dazed streetcar conductor. He was unhurt himself but shaken at the sight of the victim.

"We must get this wheel off his chest. I have an axe in my garage, and we can shop the tree branch from the top of the car," said Joe Martin, a neighbor. Two others rushed home to find any other tools that might help.

Half an hour later, a local ambulance, siren blaring, arrived. Two paramedics slowly lifted my father out of his seat onto a stretcher and drove to the nearest hospital.

My mother and us girls were sound asleep, but the ringing of the phone woke the household. Half asleep mother answered the phone.

"Yes, I am Mrs. Paquette. Are you saying my husband is in the hospital injured from a car accident? I need to call a taxi, I don't drive. I will be there as soon as possible!"

Barely able to talk and scared, I said, "Go, Mom, quickly! We can take care of each other."

Anita may have been the oldest, but she had a very soft voice. My strong voice always commanded attention from my sisters.

My mother's hair uncombed, still in her nightgown and sobbing, she pulled a coat from the hall closet and rushed to the door to wait for the yellow cab.

Arriving at 3:00 A.M. she grabbed the handle of the cab door and yelled to the driver, "Sacré Coeur Hospital fast! This is an emergency. Please don't talk to me!"

The emergency room at Sacré Coeur Hospital was attended in this early morning hour by two young interns. It was normally a boring shift at the suburban annex, not like the downtown hospital where action occurred night and day. The paramedics hurried to transfer their patient onto a stretcher to the x-ray room. The two interns and a nurse looked over the injuries.

"Broken nose, fractured arm, needs to be reset and wheeled to the plaster room, and nurse, clean the blood - nothing too serious," said Dr. Rosen.

Dr. Rosen enjoyed giving orders to the nurses, feeling his new power as a future doctor. Nurse Lea quickly obeyed the orders, and before wheeling my father out of the room, she turned to Dr. Rosen and a kiss in his direction. It was a pleasant non-committed affair since both had spouses. The early arrival of this new patient had interrupted their quickie sex in an adjoining room.

The x-rays complete, nurse Lea returned them to Dr. Rosen for his diagnosis.

"Definitely a broken arm and nose. I'll take care of it. Find him a bed and give him a strong cup of coffee, a cigarette, and call his wife or whomever."

My father was still half conscious, his groans did not seem strong enough for nurse Lea to be concerned about. His chest had not been x-rayed, even though the medical chart stated that the steering wheel had been chopped away from his torso.

My mother arrived at the hospital shaking, in tears. My parents had been married for fifteen years and were a very affectionate couple. My father and their children were her life, and she was completely dedicated to our needs and care. Mother stopped by the front desk and asked for the room number of her husband.

"Please wait in the reception room and the doctor on duty will be with you shortly."

Minutes dragged out to an hour. My mother was not a patient woman, especially where her family was concerned.

Pacing the hospital floor nervously, she rushed to the admission clerk and in a loud voice said, "Let me see my husband! I know that he has been here for several hours!"

As she glanced toward the end of the hallway, she could see two doctors and a nurse speaking with great agitation; the voices not loud enough for her to hear the conversation.

"How can he be dead? It was only a broken arm and nose?" asked Dr. Jones, who had been sharing the shift with Dr. Rosen.

"Now read the chart. Where are the x-rays for his chest? Did anyone think of that, nurse Lea?"

"I was only told to x-ray his arm and nose, assign a room, give him coffee and cigarettes. As I left the room, he screamed and....died! Just like that! What are we going to tell his wife?"

Mother, sensing something was terribly wrong, walked closer to the medical trio, desperately trying to hear the exchange of words. To no avail, she returned to the admissions clerk,

"What is happening with my husband? And why are these doctors standing in the hall and arguing?"

"I will page Dr. Rosen," replied the clerk, somewhat aware that this was not the hospital's best team.

"Paging Dr. Rosen," the voice echoed throughout the now deserted corridor. "Dr. Rosen, please come to the front desk."

Dr. Rosen, as an intern in his late twenties, had barely passed the qualifying exams for residency, had stayed up for several nights cramming for finals with the aid of uppers and downers. He and other students had partied much too late with the last crop of local debutantes. Paul Rosen was from a poor family and had to sign part of his career enrolled in the ROTC for scholarships. His mission in the medical field had more to do with earning a substantial living than saving lives.

"Mrs. Paquette, please follow me to a waiting room. You will be more comfortable, and may I offer you a coffee?" he asked in a strangely polite manner. "I am very sorry to inform you that your husband died suddenly due to unknown complications from the car accident. We and the staff will do our best to understand how he died and will keep you informed. His body cannot be released because an autopsy will have to be completed according to the laws of the Provincial Government in such a case."

"My God! I have five daughters to care for. Please, please check again! Are you sure he is dead?"

"I'll give you a sedative; it should help your pain. But there are papers that need your signature, and you have to verify that this is his body." Dr. Rosen was talking nervously now, knowing all too well the possibility of negligence and that his career may be in jeopardy. As he helped my shaking mother out of her chair, he suddenly felt the responsibility of this death due to his inattention to my father's fractures. But the paperwork must be completed.

My father's body would not be released by the hospital officials for more than forty-eight hours due to the questionable circumstances of his death. In the legal document, the coroner stated that Alfred Paquette was intoxicated when he collided with the electric streetcar. He was not charged for damages to the streetcar, since they could not prove who was at fault. Mother received only a small insurance settlement.

Returning home by taxi, mother rushed out of its door and went directly to the kitchen. Tears covering her face, trembling and wondering how to tell us.

"I have terrible news. Your father did not survive the car accident. Margo, I need your strength more than ever to care for your sisters. They will listen to your voice."

The Funeral

The funeral arrangements were a major task for my mother. Her parents were dead, no brothers nor sisters, and she had never developed a close relationship with her husband's family. My father was the only son of a wealthy business man, Cleophas Paquette, who lived in Aylmer, Quebec with his wife Adelina and their three daughters, Marie, Jacqueline, and Paulette. Both parents adored their beautiful son, and the sisters never objected to the lavish worship he received from them. Needless to say, his death was traumatic to everyone.

My mother was of French and German descent, brought up with a strict code of discipline, and she followed suit in bringing up her daughters. Before leaving for the funeral, she called us to a family meeting in the dining room. She explained that the only acceptable behavior would be no sobbing, no tears. All dressed in black, we boarded the limousine in silence for the final journey.

After the funeral service at St. Paul's Church on Aylmer Road, a large procession of cars followed the casket to the family plot, owned for more than 100 years by the Paquette family. They were not devout Catholics, but the name had great standing in the community nevertheless, and the priest performed his required duties.

As the immediate relatives gathered closer to the burial ground, the local priest recited the usual prayer in Latin and sprinkled holy water on the casket. My grandfather, Cleophas, had been completely silent during the entire service and watching the casket being lowered in the ground, passed out on the grassy site.

Jacqueline, the fashionable sister, screamed as she threw herself on the casket, and a crazy circus atmosphere ensued. Stunned by the performance, my mother reached for my hand and moved us away.

"Let's go home."

My parents lived well and entertained to the maximum on my father's income. Life was grand, and the tomorrows always seemed to take care of themselves. Now a single parent with five young daughters to care for, my mother would have to go to work.

A few weeks following Father's death, mother became ill, hemorrhaging profusely. Sitting on her bed, she called out, "Margo! Call Dr. Bedard. Tell him it's urgent and he needs to come to the house right away. Call my cousin Jeanne, so she can help you with your sisters."

Within hours Dr. Bedard and Jeanne were at her bedside. "It's serious. She has lost a lot of blood and seems very weak. These pills should help, but she needs rest for several days."

"I'll take care of her and the children," said Jeanne.

A few weeks later, my mother had somewhat recovered and again called us together. "Before being ill, I rented a furnished apartment. This house is too expensive. The apartment is small, but it's in a very nice building in downtown Ottawa on the third floor, no elevator...I also made arrangements with a nearby boarding school so you can all come home weekends. I made an appointment for an ambulance to move me up to the third-floor apartment on a stretcher; we can all ride together."

Only a woman like my mother would have made such arrangements in her condition. She was a caring, strong-minded SURVIVOR! I love you, mom.

Boarding School Days

It was sunny and unusually warm day for September. The red and yellow leaves were everywhere on our front lawn, and a "HOME FOR SALE" sign was bending in the autumn breeze. A reminder of a lifestyle changing all too quickly for our young family.

Fortunately my mother had a teaching degree. She previously taught in the Aylmer Elementary School where she met my father and grandfather, who were serving on the Board of Directors. Now alone with no extra income, she had a decision to make. She chose to send us to a private boarding school nearby, and Louise, a six-week-old baby, was to be cared for by a close friend while she taught at school.

The alarm clocks had been set for 7 A.M., but as we weren't too anxious to leave our comfortable beds, we had to dress quickly. I rushed to the bathroom, looking in the mirror at my long auburn curls. I grabbed the scissors and quickly cut the long hair my father had once so admired.

"Hurry up in the bathroom!" screamed my sisters. I opened the door and saw the disbelief on their faces.

"You look awful! Why would you do such a thing to your hair? Did you ask Mom's permission?" asked Anita.

Hearing the loud noises, mother rushed upstairs. Looking at the curls on the bathroom floor, her eyes teared up.

She pulled me to her chest and said, "Dad would not have wanted you to go to such extremes, but I share your pain."

Anita, the eldest, was fifteen-years-old, attractive, and blonde with blue eyes. She suffered from severe asthma, leaving her with a soft voice in contrast to my strong alto voice. Marie was also blonde with blue eyes and the most stubborn of all the sisters. Charlotte, ten-years-old, was the only brown-eyed sister, often teased that she was adopted; she had a shy personality and was mother's favorite. Louise, six-weeks-old, would be cared for by a close friend.

Mother had given birth to five daughters and one son. Born at home in the middle of the night, their first son was delivered by a close family friend, Dr. Perrier, who had recently retired due to severe arthritis in his hands. He had not given up his daily extra dry martinis taken for the pain. Dr. Perrier had birthed hundreds of babies in his lifetime and of course accepted the urgent 3 A.M. call from my father, almost hysterical because my mother was in hard labor. A nine-pound boy with red hair was delivered, and the doctor left quickly thereafter. A few hours later, the infant was crying loudly bathing in his own blood. Dr. Perrier had not properly tied the umbilical cord. My father rushed to the crib, not knowing what to do, held the baby in his arms. It was too late, his baby boy died.

Almost pulling the phone out of its socket, he called the nearby hospital explaining the urgency and told my mother, who was lying half conscious in the bed, "I'm going to find that fucking doctor and kill him."

Profane language was never used in our home. My father was out of control. He ran out of the house in search of Dr. Perrier, who was not to be found. Exhausted he decided to find a small casket before returning home. The ambulance was in the driveway, but my father told him to come back in a few hours. He wanted time alone with his son. Holding his baby in the white satin casket in his arms, he sobbed. I had never seen my father cry. He would insist that a funeral service be held, and later we buried Hector in the Aylmer family plot. The blood line of the Paquette name ended that night in 1937. Strange coincidence that years later my father would also die due to medical malpractice by a doctor.

Time to go to Wisdom Hall Boarding School. It was not a happy day, but knowing our mother's grief, we tried to be cheerful about this new adventure.

After a hearty breakfast, we all jumped in our new Ford station wagon, purchased with the small insurance claim my mother had been awarded. It was not the life she had planned so long ago, but we hoped for better days.

When we arrived at Wisdom Hall, the massive, carved entry door was partially opened. A tall nun dressed in a heavy grey gabardine robe and a strand of large brown beads with a cross formed the belt around her waist. A long starched white veil completed her uniform.

The main office was very impressive with built in walnut bookcases bearing carved religious symbols, held hundreds of books covered in rich leather. Her chair was almost throne-like, covered in blue velvet. Mother Superior, as she was called, sat behind a large and somewhat intimidating desk. She spoke with a heavy French accent.

"Please sit, Mrs. Paquette," Mother Superior directed our mother to a nearby wooden chair, very uncomfortable. "I will review our rules children. We do not believe in physical punishments, but infractions are given a ten-point scale, meaning you will not be able to visit your family for that weekend and your parents will be informed of your bad behavior."

This was the beginning of a long list of rules at Wisdom Hall:

1. Out of bed at 6 A.M., make beds immediately, blankets and sheets folded in an military way, we will show you how to make a perfect bed.

2. Individual basins are in your dorm. Do not expose your body, keep you robe on while washing. Do not linger and look at your naked bodies; it's a mortal sin.

3. Church services are held every day at 6:30 A.M. You are to be in full uniform, your head covered with a beret.

4. Breakfast at 7:30 and proceeding in file to the refectory, two by two without speaking. Never change places with another. This would be considered an infraction to the rules.

5. School hours are from 8:00 A.M. to 4:00 P.M. with an hour for lunch, an hour for recess, speaking is permitted during recess.

6. Dinner is at 5:00 P.M. followed by homework in the classroom. Questions are not to be asked to the supervisor during this study period.

7. In class when needing to answer a teacher's question, raise your right hand, wait for the teacher to call you, stand, both hands clasped, your feet at an angle (She stood to demonstrate).

8. Saturdays and Sundays are spent with your families at home, unless you have incurred infractions to the above

rules or if your family is not available to receive you for whatever reasons.

9. All your mail received here will be opened by a designated nun. This is for your protection.

After a brief goodbye to our mother, we were quickly divided and led to dormitories titled A B C D, each with approximately twenty beds. Anita and I were assigned to Dorm C, Marie and Charlotte to Dorm D. Beds were not close to one another for the nuns needed a better view to keep control of any communications between students.

My immediate roommate, Jose Carlos, was a beautiful tall girl with olive skin and deep brown eyes, as well as a very developed figure for a thirteen-year old. Her father and mother had been killed in a plane crash and her only remaining relatives to assume guardianship were two elderly aunts who never had children and were not happy about the idea of instant motherhood.

The first day was rather uneventful. We were summoned by Mother Superior to review schedules and expected behavior at Wisdom Hall.

These rules would not be easy for my sister Marie, the most undisciplined of our bunch. One afternoon during class, Marie, a slow learner, not only refused to answer the teacher's question but started to laugh, mimicking her speech. The students started giggling. Furious the teacher, Sister Therese, sent her out of the classroom telling Marie that she would be severely punished. Marie received a ten and could not go home that weekend.

That night Marie was forced to stand in a hallway closet for hours. Scared and crying, she was finally permitted to return to her dorm but denied going to the restroom. Marie wet her bed. Embarrassed, she laid quietly in the wet bed.

The morning bell rang, and as usual Sister Therese, the room warden, was standing at the door fully dressed in her grey uniform.

In a loud voice, she said, "Out of bed, everyone." Marie did not move. The nun, again thoroughly annoyed by this child, walked toward her bed, screaming, "What are you doing in bed? Not enough time in the closet?" She pulled Marie's blanket and saw the wet sheets. "I'll show you what we do with bed wetters." Sister Therese walked swiftly to a closet, took a naked rubber doll, and returned to Marie's bedside. Pulling her out of bed, she wrapped the damp sheet around Marie's shivering shoulders and hitting her with the doll said, "You will walk by the beds of your roommates, so they can see what a baby looks like at your age, and I order everyone to call you 'baby' as you go by."

Marie received a ten and did not go home that weekend either, forbidden to discuss the incident with her mother and sisters. Most students had departed Wisdom Hall for the weekend. It was very lonely for Marie, who was desperately missing her family. At bedtime the nuns marched everyone left to their dorms. Marie fell out of step from the remaining girls, and the Sister gave her a hard push.

"I hate you! I hate all of you! I want to go home!" cried Marie and ran down the stairs toward the front door. Sister Madeline, in charge of remaining students, ran after her, grabbing her by the neck and pulled her back in the room. Marie struggled; Sister Madeline kicked her in the ankles.

"We have ways to calm insubordinate girls," she said, dragging Marie toward a sink filled with water. Sister Madeline pushed her face in it, holding her down firmly by her hair. Gasping for air, Marie kept moving her head side to side.

Almost unconscious the Sister pulled her out and said, "Marie, do you now understand to obey the rules?"

Yes, she now understood their methods. Her fighting spirit was broken, and for the remaining two years at Wisdom Hall, Marie became a very silent and quiet student.

The sinking water boarding was a regular practice by the Wisdom Hall nuns but kept secret for fear of being charged by officials.

The warm summer days started to be interesting. At recess in the school yard, myself, Jose, and a few other girls hearing strange sounds from the pig pen decided to go and see about the noise.

"The hogs are pregnant," said Jose.

"I have never seen an animal born, this may be very educational, and the Sisters are taking their usual naps," I said.

Excited by this new discovery, we walked through the tall grass, jumping and pretending it was a safari.

"Come, come! This huge pig is having piglets!" Jose's voice was screaming, forgetting that we should not be near the wired fence.

"You are disgusting!" said an angry nun nearby. "This is a mortal sin watching animals in this act. Your will all be punished and go to confession on Sunday. Sister Superior will decide what fits this revolting behavior."

Needless to say we were all given not one but three tens.

We tried to explain to the nun that we all made the decision to go to the pen, but Mother Superior would not accept this. She wanted Jose to understand her powers in enforcing the rules. The Sisters of Wisdom were aware of each student's weakness in order to maintain their high standard of discipline. Knowing that Jose had been treated by a psychologist and had a fear of the dark, Mother Superior did not hesitate to pronounce the sentence...

"Jose, you will spend the night in the attic for your terrible act, and I hope that God can forgive you."

"Please, Sister, I'm afraid of the dark. I will not be able to breather. Punish me some other way."

With a stroke of her hand, the nun dismissed the other culprits.

The story was a major topic in the school. That evening as we went to our dorm, I reached for Jose's hand and whispered, "Don't be afraid up there. I'll pray for you."

Sister Madeline was waiting by the door and called out to Jose, "Are you having a conversation? I am waiting for you."

Jose stood by her bed, determined not to leave. The nun walking quickly pulled her by the arm and almost carried her up the short flight of stairs to the attic.

Throwing a sheet on the floor, she said; "This is your bed for the night. I will inform your aunts of your corrupt mind."

Screams could be heard throughout the night as our dorm was directly under the attic. I was sad and restless hearing her voice, but the worst was yet to come.

It was now 6 A.M., and I heard footsteps coming from the attic but no sound from Jose. Two nuns entered the attic and found Jose hanging by a sheet from the ceiling.

In a loud voice, Sister Madeline screamed, "This is a suicide!"

Unable to cope with the darkness, at thirteen-years-old, Jose had taken her own life.

Standing in the doorway of the church, Mother Superior announced to all, "You all should be aware that Jose was not well recently and will be leaving the boarding school today. Go to your pews, stay longer, and pray for her."

Jose's body was moved to the basement and an ambulance was called. Mother Superior telephoned Jose's aunts and informed them of her death. They were not overly grief stricken since they had been reluctant in accepting the burden of caring for a teenager in the golden years anyway.

The nuns must have sensed that for me, her death was questionable, especially her sudden departure without saying goodbye to a friend. A few days later, I was called to Mother Superior's office.

"Please sit. Your probably miss Jose not telling you of her plans. The nuns thought to help you with your pain, and since you have writing abilities, you should correspond with the son of a special friend from Haiti and benefactor to Wisdom Hall. He is referred to as Papa Doc Duvalier. We have many contacts throughout the world, and it would be important to understand their cultures. Do you have any questions?"

I was not very knowledgeable about the country of Haiti nor its politics, but it sounded fascinating to correspond with someone so far away.

"Bébé Doc," as he signed his letters, had beautiful penmanship and his letters were interesting to my boring life. I wanted to be a writer, and "Bébé Doc" excited my imagination for a possible escape to Haiti. Maybe his father was looking for a maiden wife for his son and probably made such a request to Mother Superior.

After months of asking Bébé Doc for his photo, it finally arrived at our house. My mother, like the nuns, always read our mail. He was definitely black. I had never seen a black person. When I was born with jaundice, my sister Anita thought that I was black. Mother had to buy a black doll to show her the difference in color.

Needless to say, Bébé Doc's photo was not acceptable.

My mother did not find it amusing that I had been chosen by the nuns to correspond with a black dictator's son. Furious she immediately contacted Mother Superior to end this relationship and she destroyed all his letters and photo, signed "affectueusement Bébé Doc Duvalier."

Very handsome!

The Duvalier Dynasty was an autocratic family and dictators in Haiti for almost twenty-nine years (1957-1986). Baby Duvalier became President of Haiti at the age of nineteen-years-old.

It was almost graduation day. Four girls in a private boarding school had been a financial hardship on my mother. She had to sell her jewelry and new car. The bus and taxi were our only transportation. She taught school all day and worked at a nursing home in the evenings.

Day before my graduation, a letter arrived from Wisdom Hall stating that she was in arrears and a lien would be placed on her salary unless tuition was paid immediately, or I would not graduate! How charitable.

Devasted and saddened by the lack of compassion in these nuns, mother, a very proud woman, never contacted relative or friends to help satisfy the tuition debt but did it alone.

I graduated! The family never returned to Wisdom Hall.

A Revision of Folk Dances

The Daily Standard Newspaper

December 8th, 1952

The Ontario Department of Education sponsored a week-long class in French Folklore songs and dances at the Cornwall High School instructed by Margo Paquet, a specialist in French Canadian Folklore.

The purpose of this course was to revive folklore dancing dating back to Samuel de Champlain (1608 founder of Quebec City Canada) to entertain the colonists. The dance was called "L'Ordre de Bon Temps" (The order of good cheers).

Over 200 people and students attended the Saturday final folk dance program, including visitors from several social clubs from Posdam and Massena, New York, close neighbors to Cornwall. All were wearing brightly-colored skirts and shirts. A few wore authentic "tuques" and multi colored wool sashes.

VIVE
LA CANADIENNE!
2 au 6 déc. 1952
ECOLE
ST-LAURENT
CORNWALL

THE DAILY STANDARD-FREEHOLDER, MONDAY, DECEMBER 8, 1952

Epoque Canadienne

Jacques Cartier made three voyages from France to NEW-FOUND-LAND in 1534, 1535, and 1541. More than 1,000 Indians greeted the explorer as they referred to their land as "Kanata."

Upon one of his return visits to France, Cartier brought the tallest native to prove to the King that he was in Canada, claiming the land for France.

Several years later, in 1608, Samuel de Champlain founded the settlement of Quebec City, overlooking the cliffs of the St. Lawrence River.

There was a severe shortage of women in Canada at that time. King Louis XIV sent Hundreds "Filles du Roi" (daughters of the King) on an all expense paid voyage to Quebec to marry the many soldiers still there. Happily the women were allowed to choose their husband. These women actually became more adapt in the colonies than the men in running the small business of fur trading and brandy making there at the time.

My family dates back to 1658 when Isaac Paquet, an officer in the Regiment Carignan Salieres, was the first uniformed army to sail from France to Quebec City. Did he marry a Fille Du Roi? Most likely!

The Carignan-Salières regiment was the first royal unit to be sent to Canada and over a third of its officers and men remained here as settlers during the 1660's. Its appearance is reconstructed from 1666 documents. The matchlock is shown with a plug bayonet which would make the gun useful as a pike. About a fifth of these troops are known to have had flintlock muskets. Watercolour by Francis Back (Parks Canada).

To survive the settlers turned to inventive methods for food–learning from the Indians. Each spring taps were inserted in maple trees, the sap boiled in iron or copper kettles until it formed a thick syrup and poured into pans or wooden molds. A very tasty treat!

Uncle Soap

After months and years of sadness and pain, I felt a need of including an interesting episode relating to the Paquette family when residing in Aylmer Quebec.

My grandmother, Adelina's eldest brother Joe, had left the family at age eighteen to seek his fortune in the 1896 Klondike Gold Rush in the Yukon, a northeast Canadian Territory.

Joe's favorite hangout had been the British Hotel on Main Street. The only one in Aylmer at the time, constructed in 1841. It included a large bar with the best brands of liquor, wine, and cigars.

The old stone-build hotel was a favorite place for political gatherings and local gossip. It was also the meeting place for travelers boarding the many steamships operating out of Aylmer for distant cities up and downstream. The Klondike was the topic of the day and very much interested Joe. The prospect of finding gold in the summer of 1896 caused many men to catch "gold fever." More than 100,000 prospectors travelled to the Klondike region in search of great wealth.

One day, after several beers and without discussing it with the family, he made up his mind to embark upon one of the steamboats to pursue his new adventure to the Yukon. No one had seen or heard from him since.

"Uncle Soap," as he would later be historically nicknamed, was an enterprising elderly, witty, handsome man in his late eighties. He traveled from town to town, first familiarizing himself with the stories of local middle-class families who may have lost touch with some relative and then duping them as that long-lost relative. This is how he survived with free room and board in his last years. The secret to his success was a bar of soap wrapped with dollar bills, which he carried in his back pocket, using it to offer to pay for his lodging. But how could anyone accept payment from a long-lost elderly relative?

Years had passed since my grandmother's brother Joe had left for his great adventure. One morning, sitting at the breakfast table with her husband and daughters, the bell rang, and she rushed to open the door. There stood an elderly man dressed in faded grey pants, khaki shirt, and a cowboy hat.

"Who are you? Do we know you?"

"I'm Joe, your old brother returning home from the Yukon! Remember me? It's been a long time, Adelina. How is Cleophas and the girls?"

"My eyesight is not as good as when you left. Please come in, you look tired. Everyone, this is my long-lost brother, Joe!"

After a brief introduction, my grandfather a bit reluctant to accept this stranger in the family, said, "Tell us more of this great adventure."

"Well, well, where do I begin? The Klondike Gold Rush was in a remote part of the Yukon; you can even find gold nuggets in the creeks. It's hard work, and one must be patient. Thousands of prospectors migrate to that area dragging old sacks for their finds, but unfortunately too many dishonest shopkeepers sell their wares at ridiculous prices, making life difficult."

"Before you tell us more, you probably need to rest. Tomorrow is another day. We have a room in the attic," interrupted my grandmother.

"I can only stay for a short time. Maybe I can help Cleophas with his coal business," said Joe.

Three months passed, and Joe was still living with my grandparents, but not used to physical labor, he had developed a weak heart. It was his last day, he told the family, but after lifting a large bin of coals, he fell screaming. An ambulance was quickly called, and the attendants lifted him onto a stretcher. A large wad of cash fell to the ground and given to Adelina.

"What is this cash? All one-dollar bills and it's wrapped in a bundle covering a bar of soap?"

Uncle Joe's façade was finally revealed. Months after duping his last victims, he died.

There's a New Country on the Planet

On July 1st, 1867, Canada signed the British North American Act and became a Federal State. Ottawa was the name given its capital, originally called Bytown after British Colonel John By, who developed and opened the Rideau Canal, known as the greatest engineering project in North America.

Bytown had been renamed Ottawa, an Indian name, during Queen Victoria's visit to the city. Currently there are over 100 foreign embassies there.

Along the Rideau Canal, thousands of tulips are given every year by the Royal Dutch family to show their gratitude for fleeing the Nazi occupation in the Netherlands in 1943. Princess Juliana was expecting a child, and she gave birth at the Civic Hospital to a girl, Magriet, who later became its Queen.

In 1982 Canada adopted its own constitution but remained part of the British Empire with Elizabeth II as Queen of Canada, only in a ceremonial role, not to interfere with its government.

A new flag was needed, not everyone supported the idea, but a selected parliamentary committee was appointed in 1946 to design a Canadian flag. It received over 2,600 entries, and my school was the one chosen. Our entry was a red maple leaf on a white background.

The leaf on the flag had points representing the Canadian provinces: Ontario, Quebec, Alberta, Manitoba, British Columbia, New Brunswick, Nova Scotia, Labrador, Newfoundland, Prince Edward Island.

Falling in Love

Life was good. Anita my oldest sister, enjoyed horseback riding and tennis and that's where she met a diplomat of the Canadian government, Martial Ouellette. At age twenty-two, she married him and moved to Paris. They had five children, born in different countries, whereever her husband was stationed as the Canadian Consulate.

Marie, an early hippie, married young to soldier Ben Malloy. Later, as a battered wife, she died of an illegal abortion, leaving four children in the care of a drunken father who raped his oldest daughter and spent only three months in jail. He refused to give custody of the girls to our family. Ben Malloy had served in the Korean war and returned a different man. I wonder if these boys, trained to kill, can ever return to a normal life. What a price to pay to defend one's country.

Charlotte, the shy and quiet on of all the sisters, met the son of a wealthy developer at one of my social events, Jean Bouchard. They married after several years of courtship and moved to Montreal and they had three sons.

Louise, an extrovert and social activist, married Terrence Sing, a program analyst, father, Chinese, mother, English; they had two daughters.

Myself, I worked for the federal government and was very active in French organizations in Ottawa. I was chosen with other members to attend a two-week camp at Lake Ouareau in St. Donat, north of Montreal, where educators in folklore taught us the songs and dances as they were performed by the colonists.

I was also active in Jeunesse Musicale du Canada, and my responsibility was to meet and greet the artist and bring him or her to the concert hall by taxi (I did not drive).

In late December, the performing artist was a violist "extraordinaire," Arthur Leblanc, who had been given a rare Stradivarius by the Canadian government. He had only request that for any "encores," he would require two bottles of Coke for extra energy available in the wings.

The taxi had been waiting outside the hall, and a terrible snow storm made it hard for Mr. Leblanc to open its door. He quickly placed the rare violin in its case on the seat. I rushed outside, opening the back door of the taxi, and as it was dark, I almost sat on the Stradivarius! Mr. Leblanc screamed!

While working for the Department of Defense as a clerk, I was assigned to Canadian, British, American officers, helping with confidential projects. I soon developed a close relationship with an American Colonel, Earl Lee, a divorcé. We had daily contacts at work, outside serious petting and kissing. My mother sensed that the relationship was getting too serious, so she decided to investigate Colonel Lee's background. There was an American Embassy in Ottawa, and without an appointment, Mother went there directly and asked to speak to the Personnel Officer. Shocked, Colonel Lee, who it turned out was married with two children living in upstate New York, she immediately filed for an inappropriate conduct citation with a young girl, me, and was told that action would be taken.

Colonel Earl Lee, American Air Force, would be transferred within weeks to Rome, New York. I was devasted and hurt, as Earl was in the process of getting a divorce. On our last day together, we went to our favorite restaurant on Rideau Street. I couldn't eat with tears running down my face as Earl gave me the wedding band he had purchased for me earlier.

One must understand that our family, for more than 300 years in Canada, had never seen a divorce. We were all French Catholic, and the Church forbade marrying a divorcee. My mother's religion was her source of vitality, giving her hope in her worse moments.

Remembering all the sacrifices she constantly made to give us a better life; how could I abandon her and cause her so much grief? Sadly I returned the ring to Earl.

It takes a long time to remember how one's heart had been broken.

A year later, my best friend Lucille convinced me to go to a resort, Pine Lodge, nearby. There I met a single student from Cornell University. Three months later; hardly knowing him, we were married and moved to Ithaca, New York.

Part II

Families

Sitting and relaxing in my two-story suburban home while waiting for my children to return from Pittsford Elementary School (best school in the county), Carrie, fourteen, Willie, twelve, and Julie, eight, I realized that for more than fifteen years I had become a professional volunteer, no pay.

I had become somewhat disinterested in my relationship with William, my husband. I tolerated his drinking and lack of attention to the children in exchange for the secure financial and social lifestyle he provided.

Although a graduate from the prestigious Cornell University, William changed jobs almost every three years, finding fault with the company's owners or top executives. We had already lived in three states, Pennsylvania, where Carrie was born, Connecticut, where Willie was born, and Rochester, New York, where Julie was born.

Few people would feel sorry and maybe even envious of our upscale surroundings, a beautiful home with intelligent, attractive children. William was the Vice President of a major manufacturing company in Rochester, but he had succumbed to heavy drinking over late-night Union negotiations in local bars. The money was being spent faster than it was coming in. There was a ritual after the monthly bills arrived where my husband would give the same speech.

"I'm tired of being the only one paying it all. Statistics now show wives are working - for now money! Get a job!"

I enjoyed our home, living in this middle-class neighborhood, being there to greet the kids when they came home from school, driving them to music classes, little league, gardening, volunteering...I made home my career and loved it all.

I don't like the term "housewife" and "homemaker." I prefer to be called "domestic goddess;" it's more descriptive (Roseanne Barr).

The reality of our financial status was a fact that I had to accept. My husband's salary had not kept pace with the accelerated cost of living. I had no choice! How does one go back to the work force after fifteen years of absence? I was scared. Feverishly I started going through the Sunday newspaper looking for part-time jobs. Suddenly there it was, "John Robert Powers Modeling School, part-time counselor with experience in pageants urgently needed."

My volunteer work had included all phases of the Junior Miss Pageant. I was a judge throughout New York State for local pageants and I had done some modeling myself. Do I dare call? (Playing it safe, means I don't was to grow anymore. Author unknown).

Determined to prove to my husband my capability, I nervously dialed the phone number listed.

A male voice answered, "John Robert Powers Modeling School. Jack Verk."

"I'm answering your ad for someone experienced with pageants. My name is Margo Tarr. I served on several pageants, including the Junior Miss Pageant sponsored by the Rochester Chamber of Commerce and…"

Jack Verk interrupted, "I'm interested in your experience. When can you come in for an interview?"

"Tomorrow"…was I too eager?

"Tuesday if good, 10 A.M.? The office is at 100 East Avenue, second floor above Madelon Furs."

I was shaking. I must not tell anyone, especially my husband, in case I don't get the job. Who would hire a woman who has not held a job in fifteen years? What should I wear? I thought that my best color was blue and I thought I should wear a hat. Men like hats. Too excited to sleep but best to get beauty rest! Tuesday, 10 A.M. I arrived at John Robert Powers and walked up the large staircase to the second floor. The main door opened to a large, lavish French provincial décor, a large sculptured desk, and a window covered with blue velvet drapes. Very impressive!

The interview went well. President Verk, a tall blonde man with piercing blue eyes, seemed very interested in my background.

"I like your hat," he mentioned. Glancing also at my body, he's flirting a bit, but I like it. I wanted to look professional, so I wore a navy-blue tailored suit, white starched blouse, and pumps. I was feeling confident.

"Can you start in a week?" he continued without hearing my answer. The process of finding contestants for Miss Rochester should be easy since we have many models to choose from and access to students at the Eastman School of music nearby. Talent is extremely important in these competitions.

I GOT THE JOB! The salary was low, but it pays – I'll have money. My life would never be the same.

ROCHESTER DEMOCRAT AND CHRONICLE   Thu

ASSISTANT DIRECTOR—JOHN ROBERT POWERS SCHOOL

Margo finds each work day stimulating because, as Assistant Director of the John Robert Powers school, she initially meets all the interesting clientele from sales clerk to psychiatrist. From that first meeting to graduation, she is an integral part of the vital force that assists the self-improvement-oriented students to realize their full potential . . . and they do. Graduates of the John Robert Powers school include such achievers as Jacqueline Onassis, Grace Kelly and Diana Ross.

Margo
Tarr

Models Etc., an off spring of the School and its many students keeps Margo busy with daily calls for modeling assignments, fashion shows, promotional work etc. etc. . . . To add a little bit more excitement to it all, she also co-ordinates the Miss America Pageant for Miss Rochester and has been active in pageants for the past eight years throughout New York State.

In 1966 when the bilingual Margo, who speaks fluent French, served as Chairman of the Junior Miss Pageant, she received the award for "Outstanding Project of the Year" from the Junior Chamber of Commerce. She was one of the few women made honorary member of the JayNcees.

This busy mother of three youngsters is greatly involved with numerous Rochester community affairs and active in civic work.

JOHN ROBERT

POWERS SCHOOL

TELEPHONE
(716) 232-7010

133 EAST AVENUE • ROCHESTER, N. Y. 14604

MARGO TARR
Ass't Director

Working Days at John Robert Powers

Within two years, I had climbed the ladder from part-time counselor to full-time Assistant director. My photograph was often in the news since the school was involved in numerous community activities. I gave lectures in make-up and wardrobe to bank employees, even Xerox requested my services.

My children were excited with my new career, especially seeing me in TV commercials. My mother was always willing to care for my children when needed.

My husband had told me to get a JOB, not to become successful and enjoy myself so much. He missed the special dinner meals, ready mix cocktails, entertaining his golf buddies...those little extras that a non-working wife could provide. He was not ready to cope with this change of lifestyle. He drank more.

The daily routine at JRP, interviewing prospective clients, scheduling teachers for classes, contacting agents for TV commercials for "our girls"... it was challenging.

I was also asked to coordinate a meeting with Nelson A. Rockefeller and the contestants for the Miss Rochester Pageant at a local political event.

A few days earlier, sitting in the waiting room of my daughter Carrie's orthodontist for braces, a nurse said in a very loud voice; "Mrs. Tarr, it's the White House calling!"

Complete silence in the room. The call was only to confirm the time and date for the meeting with Rockefeller and the contestants. It was exciting to see all the other mothers' reaction to the White House call.

There were a few memorable incidents at JRP. Our school was located adjacent to the Sheraton Hotel on East Avenue and often had break-ins through the back door. The fire escape made it easily accessible. Nothing stolen of value, petty cash, sodas, candies.

One cold winter evening, while students were attending a class, I was sitting in the front office. Hearing noises in the hallway, I jumped out of my chair.

Seeing a young black male pulling fur coats out of the closet, I screamed, "Stop, stop!"

Startled, the young thief threw the coats on the floor and ran down the stairs, opening the front door to the street. Determined to solve and end our recent burglaries, I continued the chase for half a block. Too slow I don't know what I would have done with him if I had "caught" him. I returned shivering to the office and called the police. Two young officers arrived quickly and questions the girls, flirting lightly...nothing to report, nothing stolen, all coats saved.

The most frightening experience while at John Robert Powers School was accepting a request from the mayor to help female prisoners who had almost completed their sentences. They were ready to move on in life but needed help with their appearances. I was chosen by JRP President Jack Verk to go.

This was my first and last visit inside a jail. Carefully I chose a conservative grey suit, white blouse, and black pumps to this special assignment. As I entered the designated area, a heavy white-haired police woman wearing a dark blue uniform stated that she must "frisk me."

Checking my body with a strange baton, she said, "You have a long slit in front of your skirt. We must fix that; I'll get safety pins. It doesn't take much to excite these girls."

She led me to a small totally glass enclosed room to meet the girls. Mostly in their teens, almost all overweight, some wearing clinging jersey dresses with their boobs hanging out, they were making obscene jokes and blowing bubbles with their gum.

I glanced at this misfit group getting ready to re-enter society, and in a strong voice, I asked, "If you want to look better when you leave, I will not repeat my instructions, and before I start, you must throw out your gum and sit."

Wrong way to start! Two girls stood up, lifting their metal chairs within inches over my head, were stopped by the others. Hearing the noise, the guard rushed into the room, and with her famous baton, hit the prisoners and rescued me.

There was another event I'd like to share while at John Robert Powers School, which could have been very lucrative if I did not care about my reputation in the community. It was a quiet Monday in May when a man in his sixties walked into my office without an appointment.

He sat on the provincial chair facing me and said, "My name is Jones, and I have a great proposition for you. It will make you more money than you receive here, I'm sure. Your files are filled with names of good-looking girls, and I know many wealthy men looking for dinner companions, nothing kinky. The girls would receive a fur coat from your neighbor, Madeline Furs, instead of money; all legal, and you are paid by me, a consulting fee. Interested?"

"You want me to act as a madame? Thanks, no thanks. I have three children. If they were to find out that their mother was a madame and could go to jail, no money could compensate the risk."

"You may regret this fantastic opportunity and all that money."

"Goodbye, Mr. Jones." I quickly showed him the door.

But the most exciting assignment while at JRP was a request from Zsa Zsa Gabor's company to promote a new line of cosmetics in silver-like containers. Very expensive. President Jack Verk asked me to represent the school and fly to New York to attend a one-day seminar to familiarize myself with the products. All expenses paid by Zsa Zsa.

I arrived at LaGuardia New York airport after retrieving my one black suitcase marked with large white letters, John Robert Powers School, so it would be easy for Zsa Zsa's chauffeur to identify me. A long silver limousine was stationed by the curb, and a chauffeur ushered me in. "I will drive you directly to the Hilton Hotel and pick you up tomorrow at 11:00 A.M. for your meeting with Ms. Gabor."

I enjoyed my expensive room and was anxious to meet Zsa Zsa the next day.

As I entered her penthouse office, on Third Avenue, I stood at the door almost speechless, looking at the elaborate décor: windows almost floor to ceiling, an unusual large plexiglass desk, crystal chandelier above, chrome chairs, a huge painting of Ms. Gabor in a carved silver frame, and wall-to-wall grey shag rug.

She greeted me with her thick Hungarian accent, smiling; she introduced me to the CEO of the newly formed company.

"He will show you and instruct you on how to use my products, all on display in the adjoining room."

I sat at a small desk with a large mirror, removed my makeup, and applied her new cosmetics. Great! My skin looked radiant. Unfortunately her creams and powders were in very expensive silver-toned containers, not priced for the average consumer. A promotion for a free twenty-minute consultation at a major drugstore in Pittsford, New York was very disappointing. All the clients were expecting to see Zsa Zsa, not me. A year later, her cosmetic company filed bankruptcy.

Zsa Zsa is here!

And her elegant cosmetic collection.
The glamour secrets of one of the world's
most exciting women are here. And we've got them.

Margo Tarr
Zsa Zsa's own Beauty Consultant will be here
FRIDAY, NOVEMBER 5, 10 AM TO 4 PM
to bring you free beauty advice on:
Make-up, Skin treatment, Beauty aids

Call now for your 20 minute consultation appointment

FREE GIFT

WITH ANY PURCHASE OF ZSA ZSA'S PRODUCT
YOU WILL RECEIVE
A STUNNING LIP DESIGN KIT—A $9 VALUE

Who Will Sparkle as 'Miss Rochester'?

Margot Tarr, coordinator,

D&C Photo by Naomi Lasdon

The Pageant

Several weeks later, while working at John Robert Powers School, we interviewed and chose fifteen contestants for the pageant. A place for rehearsals was needed, and through my many contacts from my volunteer days, a small vacant theater was made available.

Luncheons and social teas were scheduled to evaluate "our girls." The local press was informed of these events and covered them well.

Off stage the music productions were under the direction of the Assistant Director of the Eastman School of Music. The contestants were ready to perform. The mayor and other officials were in attendance. Jerry Carr, a local TV personality, was the M.C.

Judges had been selected according to their social status in the community and given their instructions in rating the contestants by their talent, looks, and wardrobe. The most prominent judge, Germaine Lambert, in her 70's had written several books on fashion and was certainly an asset to our task.

The performances were a success. I collected the judges' ballots and was shocked! The favorite, a student from Eastman School, 5'8", exceptionally tall blonde with a soprano voice and a favorite, was given a low score! Mrs. Lambert's sight had been failing from cataracts, unknown to me. She selected the wrong winner, the shortest contestant of all who had recited a poem in the talent competition. Too late.

Standing at the microphone, Mrs. Lambert announced, "Miss Tina" is our new Miss Rochester!"

The remaining judges were in disbelief and did not applaud. A silence fell over the audience.

As she sat down, realizing her mistake, Mrs. Lambert apologized profusely to me and the other judges. They were not impressed.

On stage President Verk crowned the new Miss Rochester and presented her with two dozen roses and gave me yellow roses (my favorite) for an outstanding pageant.

Our chances of winning the Miss New York State title would be very grim.

Leaving the theater, Jack Verk pulled me aside and whispered, "Let's you and the committee go to the Sheraton where I am staying and relax. We deserve it."

His black Cadillac was parked near the hall entrance; me and the other four jumped in. The hotel was next door to the Powers School. As we entered, loud piano music was playing in the bar.

"Champagne! Bottles of champagne for all!" shouted Jack.

I seldom drink, but with half a bottle in my hands, all inhibitions were gone. Joe, a dark-haired Italian and in-house musician, started playing a recently popular song - the Chicken Dance. I cannot sing, but I could dance.

Shoes off I jumped on the grand piano, and yes, I did the chicken dance with the crowd screaming, "MORE, MORE, MORE!"

I do not remember awakening almost naked in the hotel bed with Jack with some of my clothes on the floor...did we have sex? I didn't want to know.

I screamed, "Jack, wake up! It's 6 A.M. You need to drive me to the theater. I left my car there!"

The station wagon was still in the parking lot, no ticket thank God. I drove quickly home. My mother had been staying with us for the past few weeks. She was waiting furiously.

"Where have you been? It's 7 A.M.! I don't want to know! Thank God your husband is still asleep!"

Olean, New York

The City of Olean had been chosen to host the Miss New York Pageant, and I assumed the mayor had a great connection with officials since Olean was only a small town and not well known.

The first European to come to the area was an explorer from Canada, Joseph de la Rochelle. Later the "Sullivan Expedition" established the first road of what later became Olean.

Having been chosen for the New York State Pageant, Olean experienced a boom in their economy. Local residents, excited about a live TV show, volunteered to help wherever needed. Chaperones from their community were to assist the candidates and agree to spend one week in Olean to attend rehearsals, interviews, dress fittings, and makeup sessions.

My mother had accepted to care for my children and husband during my absence.

Throughout the week of rehearsals, there were rampant rumors that a national activist female group would burn their bras on TV after cutting cables to protest the exploitation of women. The media added to this frenzy, spending hours in airtime promoting the rumors. Nothing happened; no bras were burnt, no cables cut.

Security was added, including new rules: contestants and chaperones were not to leave their rooms, except to go to rehearsals.

The pageant went on as planned. No surprise, our "Miss Rochester" placed fifth in the competition.

As I sat motionless at a nearby table reserved for chaperones and families, I was bored. Suddenly I felt the stare of a very handsome stranger across from me with sad blue eyes.

He reached out a hand, "My name is Al Machen, and this is my daughter Sara. I'm divorced with three children and I speak German."

"My name is Margo, chaperone for Miss Rochester, work at John Robert Powers Modeling School, have three children, and speak French." We both laughed at this instant bio.

"I love your deep voice. A female Bing Crosby?" he asked.

"No, can't sing a note. Always wished for a high-pitched voice since most of my teachers had me read morbid poems in class."

If someone had told me how drastically my life would later change after shaking hands with this stranger, maybe I would have run.

"Would you like to join me and my daughter for dinner? The hors d'oeuvres are not very filing here, and there is a great restaurant nearby...you already know everything about me!"

I hesitated, but since he was including his daughter, I figured I would be safe.

It was great food at the Marlin, and as we continued small talk about the pageant, I began to relax. A great release after an intense week of contestants tryouts and the pageant itself.

Sara, sensing some interest between her father and myself, said, "Please excuse me, I have friends waiting, and they can give me a ride home."

She kissed her dad on the cheek and waved goodbye to me.

Al moved closer. "It's a beautiful evening, and I heard that chaperones are not leaving until tomorrow. How about a nightcap at my favorite pub?"

Dare I accept? It was impossible to resist those deep blue eyes.

"Only one drink. I have to get back before the curfew," I insisted.

We drove in his long red Lincoln convertible and stopped at a nearby lake in a very secluded area. Obviously Al had forgotten about his favorite pub.

Putting his arms around my shoulders and kissing my neck, he said, "You must be exhausted."

Stroking my hair, he pulled my face close to his, and feeling no objection, he kissed my lips. In a very sexual embrace, I felt my resistance melt away. I was once told by a Franciscan priest that the lips are the most sensual part of the body.

"Lips create an unflagging urge throughout the whole human body and are very powerful." His face flushed as he said the words.

Al continued kissing me for what seemed like hours, then finally managed to pull me over on his lap. Stroking my thighs and breasts and pulling my strapless dress down to my waist. I tried to pull away, saying, "I don't usually cheat on my husband. Only once with our attorney...."

"Do you want me to stop?"

It had been months since my husband and I had had sex. His heavy drinking and bad breath didn't help create many intimate moments.

If happiness is an interval between periods of unhappiness, this was it!

The car radio was playing my favorite song, "I want to know what love is." I felt transported, alive and wanting more.

"Do you want me to continue?" asked Al softly.

"Yes, yes yes!" I had never had an orgasm before; it was electrifying, an out of body sensation. And what an erection! It felt like it was penetrating my whole body...incredible!

"I must get back to the hotel. The sun is coming up, and the contestants are probably getting ready to leave."

Should I regret this moment? Should I have walked away from this handsome stranger not knowing the future impact he would have on my life?

A long-distance relationship with Al continues. Fortunately Buffalo, New York, where he maintained an apartment during his working days, was only seventy-five miles from my home in Rochester. On weekends he would go to Olean to be with his daughters and son since he had been awarded full custody from his alcoholic ex-wife, now living with her mafia boyfriend only a few doors down the road.

At age eighteen, Al was offered the role of Tarzan by Hollywood, refused.

Divorce

Almost a year now at John Robert Powers Modeling School, still excited about my work and the publicity.

Our home life had worsened. My husband and I seldom spoke, not meaningful conversations, refusing any social invitations. He drank too much but still played golf every weekend with his old buddies, almost no contact with our children

It was a cold winter evening, sitting in the family room, the fire in the fireplace was almost out, and William was watching his favorite hockey team on TV, smoking a cigarette, sipping his third scotch...

I walked in and said, "I want a divorce."

"Okay," he responded, as if expecting this announcement. "Sit down, we need to talk. I have been offered a great job as VP in Cincinnati, Ohio...more money."

"I want a divorce, not a move to Cincinnati, wherever that is."

"Please hear me out. I don't know if I would be offered this opportunity if the Chairman knew we were in the process of a divorce. Would you consider moving there for only one year since the state of New

York requires a year after filing to grant a non-contestant divorce anyway? You can have it all, proceeds from the house, car, whatever you want. If agree, let's make a list, review it, submit it to an attorney for final draft…we can save a lot on legal fees. Do you know an attorney with all your contacts?"

"I need to sit down and think this over. Yes, possibly I know a lawyer, George Pappas. I did volunteer work for his campaign for Congress." Remembering what a joke his campaign had been, not really wanting to win since his opponent was a well-known and liked politician, he was sure to win.

"Why are you running against this Republican?" I remembered asking. The answer shocked me.

"I don't want to win, need the publicity and all the money we are going to raise."

The night of the election, George had rented a large suite at the Holiday Inn in downtown Rochester. Volunteers were at least rewarded for their efforts, champagne was flowing, great hors d'oeuvres, good music. I was wearing my favorite silk Kelly Green dress. George pulled me into the adjoining room, almost ripping my expensive dress.

"I just wanted to thank you," he whispered. Having had too much champagne, I didn't resist. Once again I hadn't had sex in months and I figured you owe me, George!

Moving to Cincinnati

Looking back at my very stupid decision to move to Cincinnati so that my husband would be given a VP position, I still fail to understand the logic of it all, the impact on my children, new schools, new doctors, new friends. However, this is a type of dedication that was expected by my generation.

Later I learned from one of his co-workers that he had asked for that position, probably hoping the move away from Rochester could save our marriage.

When a marriage is in trouble, on the verge of divorce, moving to a strange city away from relatives, friends, and career (mine) was not the best solution. Why, why, why, did I agree?

The company offered to buy our Pittsford home at a fair market price and paid the mortgage, so we accepted. Again a stupid decision. Thirty days later, too soon to say goodbye to my many friends, the Mayflower movers were at the door.

Sitting alone on the front porch, the children spending a last day at their schools, I cried, but remembering the large proceeds of the sale (more than $10,000), more money than I had ever had in my possession, I cheered up a little. Money doesn't make one happy, but it can quiet the nerves!

It was time, reservations were made on Delta airlines to fly to Cincinnati with our three children, my husband remaining there. At the company's expense, a lovely hotel suite was reserved as our temporary residence while searching for a new home.

Arriving early afternoon at the airport, with three children behind me, I went to the baggage claim to retrieve our many suitcases with help from a porter. Standing at the curb waiting for a taxi, I noticed the many cars with Kentucky license plates.

"My God, I'm in the wrong state!" almost screaming.

Laughing a bystander said, "Yes, you are in Kentucky, but it's also what we call Greater Cincinnati. The airport lies in the area of Northern Cincinnati and Kentucky. Politicians had agreed on purchasing the land in Kentucky if the airport would be named the The Cincinnati Airport."

Driving towards downtown, our children's faces against the window for a better view of the city, Willie screamed, "Look! Decorated pig statues on the sidewalks!"

The taxi driver laughed, "I can explain." His chest bursting with pride, he said, "My city was nicknamed Porkopolis dating back to the 19th century when it was the meat packing industry for the whole country! Pigs roamed the streets! It's also known as the Queen City of the West. We also have a specialty food," he continued, impressed with his own knowledge, "it's called Skyline Chili, spiced with cinnamon served over spaghetti, topped with cheese. It takes time to develop a taste, but soon you will love it!"

Sounds terrible, I thought.

I had chosen a northern suburb, newer townhomes directly on a golf course, hoping William would teach his son golf...no, he was too busy trying to impress his new partners with his great score. Willie never did learn the game.

Boxes piled up in this three-bedroom townhome. I had no intention of completely unpacking, after all it was a temporary move.

There were many urgent tasks to give my full attention to. I wanted to meet with my children's new teachers, doctors, dentists to help establish some sort of comfort in their lives.

Where do I begin myself? My career in Rochester had given me a fair share of identity and publicity. I felt lost.

Cincinnatians, I was told, are rather provincial, a very German town that once had its own German newspaper.

A few weeks later, bored, I contacted a local employment agency, re-wrote my resumé, and made an appointment for an interview. The agent made a few calls while I waited, and immediately he scheduled an appointment with a client from a trade association.

"Can you be at their office next Friday?" he asked me.

"YES, YES, YES!"

The office of the Cincinnati Board of Realtors was an impressive building. A secretary ushered me directly to the CEO's office.

"My name is Frank Rogers, please sit down. I read your resumé. You obviously can work with groups of people, important on this job."

He was a tall attractive man in his fifties, but his strong Alabama accent made it difficult for me to understand. I had to pay close attention to the words as if I was lip reading.

"The title of this position is Director of Public Relations, and the editor of our monthly newsletter, also to coordinate all social functions. You would serve on seven committees with selected volunteers representing their real estate companies. These agents are not always easy to control; our total membership is now at 4,000."

"A very challenging position," I replied. "I have never edited a newsletter."

"I will be there to help you...interested? Let me show you your corner office."

It was medium-size with windows, a large office desk, swivel chair, two leather guest chairs, built in file cabinets, not plush like my office at John Robert Powers School but functional.

"Your secretary, Jane, is very efficient. Her desk is next to your door."

I nodded, "Anxious to work with you, Jane."

Shaking hands with CEO Rogers, I gladly accepted.

With his daily guidance and support, I was hard at work, editing a newsletter for the first time in my life, "The Realtor." My first Christmas message created quite a controversy. I was only trying to prove my knowledge of facts.

"You ruined my Christmas!" screamed some members. A few others wrote SHIT across the front page and threw the newsletter on my desk. I soon realized this was an easy group to offend.

Season's Greetings

from Officers, Directors & Staff

A
CHRONICLE
OF CHRISTMAS

Christmas is probably the oldest holiday season in the world, begun ages before the Christian era.

The ancient Persians observed the birth of Mithra, god of light, on December 25 — Was Christ born on December 25? Early church scholars favored other dates. Some modern scholars believe the first Christmas may have taken place as late as April. But, to ease the conversion of their followers from paganism to Christianity, the first Popes changed many traditional pagan ceremonies into Christian rites instead of abolishing them outright. Pope Julius I in 350 A.D. proclaimed December 25 as the date of the Nativity, probably because earlier pagan sun-worshippers observed that day as the birthday of the sun. It was also the time of the Roman Saturnalia, when Saturn, the god of agriculture, was honored with feasts, gift exchanges and revelry.

Evergreens and mistletoe were important in pagan rituals, but the Christmas tree with decorations is a fairly recent invention. It began in Alsace and the Black Forest: Martin Luther is credited with being first to bring a lighted one indoors. It spread throughout Germany during the Napoleanic Wars, and to England in 1841, when Prince Albert gave one to Queen Victoria.

German Professor at the College of William and Mary, Dr. Charles Minningerode, set up and decorated one of the first recorded Christmas trees in America. He did it for a children's party in the St. George Tucker House, still standing in Colonial Williamsburg. He and the Tucker children gilded nuts and strung popcorn and colored paper to hang on the branches, along with tiny baskets packed with bonbons and a verse. A gilded crown topped the tree. The sliding doors were closed until the professor lit the candles.

The Yule-log, like the candles and their electrical replacements, is a sacred-flame device in honor of the sun. Vikings brought it to England and various parts of Europe, even as far as Greece. The huge cedar log was kindled on Christmas Eve, and no one worked as long as it lasted. Slaves in the Old South were accused of soaking the log in water, so it would burn slowly and last beyond the usual six or seven days.

The first Christmas card was designed by a 16-year old engraving apprentice, William Egley, in 1842. For his montage of revelers, dancing couples and skaters, young Egley coined the still - popular greeting "A Merry Christmas and a Happy New Year to you!"

I was responsible for promoting and coordinating large social events; quite a task with a membership of 4,000. The most prestigious award was given once a year to the top fifty sales leaders. It was called "The Million Dollar Club," and they would be presented with Oscar statuettes. Almost 900 members would attend with their companies, held at the Hall of Mirrors at the Netherland Hotel. I had spent days assigning members at specific tables. I did not know members would have the audacity to switch names on these tables...Worst yet a major company had bought the space on the hotel marquee, naming only their sales leaders and company name. What a nightmare! Members were asking ME how to get the sign removed, but I was helpless.

The Ethics Committee of the Board fined the broker $700.

I enjoyed editing and writing the CBR Newsletter, interviewing celebrities, such as the new Ambassador to Switzerland, Mr. Marvin Warner, a former member of our Board.

Realtor®
Ambassador Marvin Warner

MARGO TARR, Editor

**A man at ease with himself and the world,
ready to serve his government** . . .

"Possible, but difficult, due to the inflated const
tion costs, regulations, zoning and land use. In
opinion, however, real estate is still the best inv
ment, the number ONE! The market for home ow
ship, whether single or married, will continue stror
and stronger — it gives the feeling of security
belonging — land is the staying power. The h
concept has been inbred in the English and Amer
system of living. Condominiums have not been as e
accepted in Cincinnati, but will continue to grov
popularity — it's a necessity in today's market du
the rising cost of land. Around the Cincinnati area,
best land investment is probably in the eastern p
such as Clermont County. Especially with the c
pletion of I-275, land will increase in value. Nortl
Cincinnati, land is very expensive.

There seems to be a move of younger families f
the city to the country, by-passing the suburbs and
suburbanites moving back to the city. Prices of hoi
will rise in the country.

Apartments should become more and more valu
as housing becomes more critical. However, due
rising utility costs, these units should have sepa
meters. By 1980 we will look at today's prices and
them very low! Today's $15,000 salary will be
equivalent to $67,000 by the year 2,000!

This is the greatest nation and Americans all h
a responsibility toward this country. With the excep
of family and health, politics should be the grea
concern to everyone, we are too prone to leave poli
to someone else. It effects us daily. This country g
us so much, WE MUST GIVE SOMETHING BACK
RETURN!"

"There should always be new goals to achieve, otherwise a man becomes
too self-satisfied and looses his SNAP, SIZZLE and POP," says Realtor®
Marvin Warner, member of the Cincinnati Board of Realtors® and newly
appointed AMBASSADOR TO SWITZERLAND, in an interview with Editor
Margo Tarr.

"I feel that my many years in the real estate industry have prepared
me for my post as Ambassador," continued Marvin Warner. "In real estate,
a salesman must learn to be a lawyer, an accountant, a public relations
specialist, be aware of the economic trends of this country, the state and
local politics, zoning and public agencies in order to be successful in his
profession.

There has been and continues to be changes in the licensing of real
estate salesmen. However, I am not convinced that a degree in real estate
is the answer to professionalism, it doesn't hurt. Character and ethics are
more important — we don't need to legislate more education, salespersons
should make an effort toward self-study and industriousness. Lawyers must
pass bar exams for a license, but not all are successful in their profession
even with a degree," said Warner.

"It has been stated," commented Margo Tarr, "that the basis of almos
fortunes in this country has been in real estate. Do you believe, Mr
rner, that it is still possible to accomplish this goal?"

photos: Margo Tarr

The American Legion performed as the color guard and 23 other veteran groups were represented. The Mayor the VA Director, families and friends were all in attendance.

Let's Green America

Every year The Cincinnati Board of Realtors donated hundreds of trees to be planted along the highways to help reduce pollution.

Serving as Chair on the "Let's Green America" committee, I recommended a more patriotic gesture that year, to commemorate the eight servicemen who died in the 1980's attempt to rescue American hostages held in Iran. Interested, President Jimmy Carter negotiated the release of the fifty-two hostages, and they were freed as the new President, Ronald Reagan, took office and the credit. It was important that a lot of publicity should be given to the planting of these eight trees at the VA Hospital honoring these fallen soldiers.

The American Legion performed as color guard, and twenty-three different veteran groups were represented. The Mayor, the VA Director, families and friends were all in attendance.

I could not have had a better setting: Hollywood style, drizzling rain, standing on a small hill while a soldier played his bugle. It was very emotional. As I was leaving, I heard strong clapping from the hospital windows and could actually see tears.

"Thank you for remembering. We are so often forgotten," said a recent amputee.

Marriage License

While working at the Cincinnati Board of Realtors, we often shared general meetings with The Saving & Loan organization since our industries had similar interests.

I met the CEO of one particular banking industry, Dan Griffith IV, where we often celebrated after these meetings at a great bar-restaurant in Mt. Adams, a suburb of Cincinnati. We soon became close companions.

Dan Griffith was a graduate from Tulane University and active in many civic and social associations, including The American Society of Executives in Washing, D.C., the prestigious Ohio Society, and a member of the commercial committee of the Cincinnati and Kentucky Board of Realtors, and others.

A special event that we attended was at the Kelly Farm, a member of the Ohio Society. These wealthy farmers were asked to participate in a new venture with "beefalo," a cross-breed of domestic cows and bison (or buffalo).

Fifteen beefalos were sent from Texas to the Ohio farm. Beefalo steaks were a staple in Texas. We were served a dinner of beefalo steaks, cooked on a grill and so incredibly succulent and tender; never had I tasted such delicious meat. The Ohio Society of farmers were not interested yet.

I especially enjoyed going to the Kentucky Derby in Louisville, Kentucky, held every year the first Saturday in May. The Griffith family were longtime Kentuckians and had held VIP seats for years. Wearing a large colorful brim hat, I would only place small bets. It was always exciting to cheer for whatever horse I had chosen for the Derby.

Dan and I often visited his only aunt in Owensboro, Kentucky, an interesting town with an arts center, a riverfront plaza, and an international bluegrass music museum.

Dan and his sister Elaine Griffith were heirs to a soybean farm in Owensboro, more than 500 acres. Their father, a judge, had raised them since their mother had left with a young lover, never to return.

Dan and I did not marry. I still regret ending our three-year relationship with a phone call; too many unsurmountable issues, mostly with Dan and alcohol. My daughter Julie was devastated by my decision as she thought of Dan like a father. I must have hurt him badly.

Dan Griffith IV was divorced with one daughter, Leslie. He doubted his paternity but never took a blood test to confirm it. We dated for several years. Dan's sun sign was Libra; they don't make quick decisions. However, our engagement was published in the local newspaper and triggered a series of harassing phone calls from his neurotic and vengeful ex-wife. There were as many as fifteen calls in one night. Dan finally contacted the FBI to stop these calls that were making life miserable for all concerned.

He decided to schedule another custody hearing for his daughter so that she could be removed permanently from her mother's care.

Impatient for answers from the court, he drove to Atlanta where they lived and waited near the school yard. He convinced his daughter to return to Kentucky with him.

Our wedding was planned for August, and Leslie would remain with my family until other arrangements could be made. But her maternal grandmother had stayed in contact with her and persuaded Dan to let her spend a few weeks at her summer home.

As agreed, after two weeks, Dan called her grandmother to say he was returning for his daughter. Arriving at the summer home, no one was there. They must have left in a hurry, he thought, because her favorite rag doll was on the floor. Obviously kidnapped by her grandmother or mother, he contacted the local police, showing her photo. He drove around town for several days. No luck.

Dan returned to my condo, still holding the rag doll, not talking. He lost contact with his daughter for several years. Heavy drinking became his escape. Later he became convinced that he was being followed by local and state police, even the mob. Why would an ordinary citizen with no past connections to organized crime be followed, harassed, and threatened by these people, I had asked him. No answers.

He continued to pursue the answer to this question across fifty states and Europe.

Another important event for associates was also held once a year; no awards, just a fun evening at the Beverly Hills Supper Club in Southgate, Kentucky. The club was situated high on a hill overlooking Cincinnati, plush with enormous chandeliers, velvet draperies, and red carpeting.

Beverly Hills was known for featuring top Hollywood stars, such as Frank Sinatra, Dean Martin, Carol Channing, and many more. It was a full house that evening. Robert Goulet was featured, and I had front seat tickets from the owners since the Realtors were such great customers. My best friend Diane and

I decided to have an early dinner at the Drawbridge Inn, where most of the stars stayed before performing at Beverly Hills. Later, standing in line to pay our dinner bill, standing in front of me was Robert Goulet.

Do I dare ask in French, "Are you really Robert Goulet?"

"I love your voice, will you be singing my favorite song, 'La Mer?'"

He smiled, and looking directly at me, he sang the first verse of La Mer in French.

"La mer qu'on vont dancer a des reflets d'argent."

Everyone in the room applauded.

Beverly Hills owner told me if I returned the next evening, he would introduce me to him. Because of a terrible storm the next night, I couldn't go! Sorry.

Beverly Hills Supper Club fire was like a warzone. The most significant and critical event held a few months later, May 28th, 1977 at Beverly Hills Supper Club, will never be forgotten.

The Realtors Association, The Savings and Loan League, relatives and friends were celebrating a new type of mortgage, the "adjustable rate." Offered for the first time ever by banks to buyers, this option would make it easier for people (families) to purchase a home.

Almost 875 people were attending the performance of John Davidson, host of Hollywood Squares. It was a sellout.

Immediately as he appeared on stage, someone screamed, "Fire!" Within minutes the room was engulfed with smoke and fire, only one exit door to the outside.

"Get on the floor!" screamed a voice through the smoke.

I threw my body on the floor, wrapped my shawl around my face, and crawled as quickly as I could toward the only exit I knew, stumbling over bodies I ran outside. Shaking and crying, I stood, not remembering where I had left my car.

In a loud voice, I said, "It's a blue convertible – it should be easy to find!"

Minutes went by when a stranger suddenly appeared. "Let's go through the rows of cars....Found it!"

I believe in angels.

According to the press, 165 died that night, mostly from smoke inhalation. The bodies were taken to the Military Fort in Ft. Thomas where a temporary morgue was set up. After months of investigating, it was concluded by officials that the cause of fire had started due to electrical problems inside the walls. It was the deadliest night club fire in U.S. history.

The news of the fire exploded on TV and radio. I hugged my children as soon as I got home, called Al, and barely able to speak I asked, "Can you come to Cincinnati? I need you."

Al said, "You were so lucky! I am so happy you are well. Let's spend the weekend in Cincinnati. I'll make a hotel reservation near your home. Get a babysitter."

A few days later, Al arrived at the Ramada Inn. I was impatiently waiting in the lobby. At the sight of him, I threw myself in his arms and kissed him. I didn't care who might be watching.

"I reserved a suite thinking you might need space." Barely through the door, Al almost ripped my clothes off, and we made love for hours,

"Enough for now?" he asked. "Let's go to the dining room. I'm famished."

After the steak dinner and my favorite bourbon drink and feeling relaxed, I was able to recall some details of the evening at Beverly Hills Supper Club. Al's presence seemed to ease the pain of remembering.

Beverly Hills Supper Club fire

Dr. Henry Heimlich Benefits

Near the Realtors' office in Cincinnati is a small deli, only a bar, no tables, frequented by area workers. Dr. Henry Heimlich and myself were regulars and advertently had conversations about real estate, politics, and food. His wife, Jane Murray Heimlich, daughter of Arthur Murray, wrote several books, including the widely acclaimed *Homeopathic Medicine at Home.*

The Heimlich Institute is an internationally recognized non-profit medical research facility located in Cincinnati, Ohio. Founded and directed by Dr. Henry J. Heimlich, the Institute is dedicated to "Benefiting humanity through health and peace." Present research involves cancer, AIDS, cystic fibrosis, and emphysema.

Dr. Norman Vincent Peale said Dr. Heimlich is the man responsible for saving more lives than any other living American. The Heimlich Maneuver, an emergency treatment for choking and drowning victims, became universally known, but many people are not aware of the Heimlich Institute's other life-extending developments. For example the Micro-Trach, a tiny plastic tube, allows victims of emphysema and cystic fibrosis to breath easily using a small portable oxygen container. Former astronaut

Neil Armstrong, Dr. George Rievescl, and Dr. Edward Patrick participated in this research in the mid-seventies.

The Heimlich Chest Drainage Valve saved hundreds of lives during the Vietnam War and has since helped thousands of people following lung and heart surgery. The Heimlich operation for replacement of the esophagus made medical history as the first total organ replacement ever performed and is widely used to overcome birth defects and cancer.

After twenty-five years of research, the Heimlich Institute was progressing toward a major goal: treatment of cancer with malaria hyperthermia. A patient treatment center has been established at the Nation Cancer Institute in Mexico City. The Centers for Disease Control (CDC) in Atlanta is working with the Heimlich Institute to establish this cancer treatment in the United States.

Currently a treatment for AIDS victims has been researched and plans for patient treatment are being developed.

The Heimlich Institute is now headquartered in Cincinnati, a city with a tradition of medical breakthroughs. When offers were extended to the institute to relocate, a group of dedicated volunteers for the Heimlich Institute organized the first Save-A-Life Dinner in the fall of 1986.

I co-chaired the first Save-A-Life event at the Netherland Plaza with Nick Clooney as Master of Ceremonies, a writer for the Cincinnati Post Newspaper and father of actor George Clooney. The second Save-A-Life benefit titled "Le Bal Intime," a more formal event, black tie, was held at the Peterloom Estate in Indian Hills, a wealthy Cincinnati suburb. Dr. Henry Heimlich dies in 2016 at the age of ninety-six-years-old.

Harry Whittaker, left, and Margo Tarr, center, talk with Dr. Henry Heimlich at a recent fest at Whittaker's Grandin Road home to plan 'Le Bal Intime' at Peterloon Oct. 17 for the benefit of the Heimlich Institute.

Socko and Me

For several years, I had an on and off relationship with a prominent politician, Socko Wiethe, Chairman of the local Democratic Party, well-known for his early athletic years playing football for the Detroit Lions and coaching the University Bearcat team and drinking.

One afternoon, September 26th, my birthday, he called me and said in an agitated voice, "Meet me at 4 P.M. at the Normandie restaurant, I have something urgent to discuss with you."

The Normandie was a favorite by locals for its steak dinners and its unusual décor; peanut shells covering the floors and on tables for all you can eat.

I arrived on time. Socko was waiting to order. "I talked to my brother, the priest, and he informed me that I could marry a divorcee if you obtain an annulment from the Church. Interested?" He looked directly in my eyes and waited for an answer.

What a strange proposal of marriage!

"An annulment would make my previous marriage invalid and my children all illegitimate. As much as I care for you, I cannot do this to my children, make them illegitimate. They would never forgive me. We can still remain great friends. Sorry."

He pulled my hand and gave me a sapphire and diamond ring as a birthday present and smiled. For several years we continued seeing each other, attending many social and sports events.

The sadist moment in both our lives was when Socko was forced to resign the Chairmanship of the Democratic Party. His health had deteriorated; age, drinking, and a severe head injury when hit by a car during a political trip in California had done him in. He was sent to a rehab center by his four children, who had filed for guardianship of his estate, estimated at $1.5 million. The court also appointed a family attorney to represent him. It made headlines in many papers in the country. Reading the story, I cried. He deserved better.

A Salute to Socko

The Democratic Party and many volunteers planned a testimonial dinner as a "Salute to Socko" to be held at the Cincinnati Convention Center.

A few days before the event, I visited Socko at the rehab and was shocked to discover that this family had not informed him of the testimonial dinner, and he was expected to give a speech. Did his children purposely not tell him, feeling guilty for having him committed and justifying to everyone that he would not be capable of giving an audible speech?

More than 300 invited politicians, families, and friends showed up. I received a personal invitation from the committee and was seated at his table. Furious with his children when he arrived, asked that they be seated elsewhere. Socko gave an outstanding speech, for one hour in his normal strong voice, thanking the party and volunteers for this testimonial. His last speech.

Socko had been admitted at the Cincinnati Jewish Hospital a few months after leaving rehab. I visited him the evening before he died, alone, breathing heavily, not speaking.

I touched his hand and said, "Thank you, Socko, for all the wonderful moments we shared." Then I left. He died at seventy-six-years-old.

John "Socko" Wiethe
A lifetime fueled by politics

The 'Socko' file

- Graduated from Xavier University in 1934.
- Taught at Roger Bacon High School, 1935-38.
- Played for the Detroit Lions, 1939-42.
- Admitted to the bar, 1941.
- Head basketball coach at UC, 1946-52.
- Unsuccessful race for Hamilton County prosecutor, 1952
- Became Democratic party chairman, 1954.
- Ousted as chairman, 1964
- Back as co-chairman, 1968.
- Seriously injured when he was struck by a car in Palm Springs, Calif., April 24, 1979.
- Survives an attempt to oust him as chairman, May 1988.
- Citing bad health, resigns as chairman, July 8, 1988.

FLORIDA

In the 1970s, the real estate market crashed, especially affected was the state of Florida.

My divorce was soon to be final; the year had arrived. I contacted my attorney for a court hearing date. I had to fly to Rochester. A non-contested divorce process, even in court, is a simple event, only one person need to be present.

As soon as I left the courtroom, I rushed to a phone to call Al. "I'm free, I feel free…let's go to Florida to celebrate!"

Al and two friends had bought a condo, real cheap, in Daytona Beach on Atlantic Avenue the year before. And I now had the proceeds from the sale of our home in Rochester in the bank. The Towers condominium had an in-house agent, and within days I signed on the purchase of a one-bedroom condo myself, overlooking the Atlantic Ocean for $25,000. It was completely furnished, and I was permitted to stay there until all the paper work was completed. A great investment. The Towers was an impressive sixteen-story white stucco building with a great "wow" effect the moment a person entered the lobby. The walls were all pale blue, including a carpeted area over white marble tile. A five food stuffed marlin fish hung on the main wall, royal blue sofas with massive oriental white/blue vases...unbelievable! It was like looking at a page from Architectural Digest come to life.

We had decided to include the children in this Florida vacation - Al had three and I only brought Julie. School was out, and the children needed to get to know each other if there was going to be a future in this relationship. Al had been awarded full custody of his three children, Gina, Sara, and Albert, since his ex-wife was an alcoholic and proven incapable of caring for their safety. Rose, his ex-wife, had threatened to kill Al on several occasions, including when entering the house late one night. She had thrown an ax at his (their) bedroom door. Fortunately he had had a major lock installed on the inside of the door. Rose and a well-known mafia boss had bought a house three doors down from their former home and kept close contact whenever possible with their children.

Before arriving at the Towers, we stopped at the closest Publix to buy food. The Towers had atwenty-four4-hour receptionist; everyone had to register, including owners, before being permitted to go to their unit. Great security!

Registration complete Al said, "Let's get settled in our separate condos, eat, and rest for the evening. It's been a long ride for all. We can meet in the morning after breakfast by the pool."

Waiting for everyone to be asleep, Al came down to my fourth floor condo, knocked four times on the door, our normal signal, and quickly opening it, I rushed into his arms.

"How about a cold vodka martini? There's liquor in this cabinet," I said.

"Yes, yes," he replied. "And let's take a long walk on the beach, the children are safe here."

The children all enjoyed the ocean, the sunny weather, and especially the trip to Disney World, which had recently opened. The rides and the park were all an unbelievable sight.

For our last day, I wanted everyone to savor the local fish, so I cooked a "paella," a recipe of fish and rice that I learned in my gourmet cooking lessons in Rochester during my "housewife" days.

Everyone seemed to enjoy the meal. Still seated at the table, Julie stood up, plate in hand, and started licking it.

Al's kids laughed, but Al turned to me shocked and said, "Please stop her."

"It's all for attention," I replied. Julie, my youngest daughter, did not want to share me with men; it was the security she needed since the divorce.

Reluctantly we had to return, crowded in a Ford van for the trip home, almost in silence. Our children were not happy to share this space. Halfway home we stopped at a nearby hotel, Holiday Inn, as we all gladly left the crowded van and rushed to the lobby.

Al booked three rooms, one for his girls, one for me and Julie, one for himself and his son.

As we started to unpack, a voice on the loud speaker began shouting, "Evacuate, there's a bomb!" Everyone ran outside. We grabbed our bags and ran. Fire trucks and ambulances arrived within minutes.

"Let me go to a pay phone and call Mom…I see a public phone near the driveway. It will only take a minute to reassure Mom," said Gina.

I could barely hear the conversation but definitely the words, "Yes, Mom, the bomb scare went okay, you did good."

"Best to go to another hotel. Let's get in the van now," said Al nervously.

Al drove Julie and I to the clubhouse in walking distance to our townhome where Carrie, Willie, and my ex-husband were staying. I did not want to call attention to our arrival. Al continued non-stop to Olean with his children sleeping most of the way.

We had agreed to wait until June when all children were out of school before having a small wedding and moving my family to Al's house in Olean, New York. His large four-bedroom contemporary home, Frank Lloyd style, two floors, featured an impressive circular black wrought iron staircase. I love the house.

Psychic Predictions

This townhome complex, on a golf course, was mostly inhabited by young divorcees, quite a different environment from our neighborhood in Rochester, New York. The clubhouse had a large bar, great gathering place for owners to meet some interesting women, all divorcees, chit chat and the ladies liked to gossip about the men.

Denise, my closest confidant, talked about a well-known psychic, "Sonya," who was often used by local police to solve crime in our area.

"We must go. I need to know more about my future plans with Al. Can you find where she lives?"

"I kept the recent news article on her great psychic abilities...let's call the newspaper or try to find it in the phone directory. Yes! Her name is listed in the White Pages!" Nervously Denise dialed the number.

A deep voice answered. "Do you do readings for the general public? We are two girls who desperately need some answers in our lives."

"Yes, you can come tomorrow at noon. I only accept donations."

"Thank you so much! My name is Denise, and my friend is Margo."

Beacon Street, where Sonya lived, was not easy to find; a low-class district with many homes desperately in need of repair, some abandoned.

The next day, we arrived at noon and knocked several times on the heavy wooden door. A tall woman with long stringy black hair and piercing brown eyes motioned for us to come in without a word.

"I do one reading at a time. Come behind this closed door." She pointed at me.

I rushed to her side, anxious to hear about my wedding plans with Al. As I sat opposite her, she held my hands, looked at me strangely, painfully.

She uttered, "An explosion, a broken wedding...do not sleep in this other woman's bed, we spirits don't approve...I am so sorry for you. Please go, this is all I can say."

My whole body was shaken as I certainly did not expect such a grim prediction.

After Denise's reading, we left quickly, placing a donation in the ashtray by the door.

In spite of her sad predictions, I rushed home and continued packing for our move to Olean. Carrie and Julie would come with me as agreed, and Willie would remain with his father in Cincinnati.

Planning Our New Home

"Can you come this weekend to discuss room arrangements and other changes needed to make this house our home?" Al was anxious to finalize all plans.

Arriving at his home in Olean, Gina was at the front door and said, "I'm not staying here, I'm moving in with my mother." She slammed the door behind her. Al had felt the resentment of our marriage but did not try to change her mind. Sara embraced me. She was happy for her father and seemed to like me.

"I made your great seafood dinner and prepared your room with satin sheets and lavender candles all over for great ambiance."

"Sounds perfect," I said. But suddenly remembered the psychic's words, "We spirits don't like anyone else to sleep in our beds."

Sara seemed to have tried very hard to make me feel welcome and comfortable; I had to accept it all. I shared my feelings about the psychic reading with Al.

"Just words; I don't believe in fortune tellers. Let's enjoy the weekend, so happy to have you here!"

Al had married Rose, now is ex-wife, after meeting her in a local bar near his office. He was not a heavy drinker; obviously Rose was. She kept ordering straight vodka with three olives, water on the side, a recipe very familiar to the bartender, as was Rose.

Wearing a very short skirt, split up the front, Rose moved closer to Al's bar seat; obviously drunk she started caressing his leg, slowly reaching his upper thigh.

"My name is Rose. Haven't seen you here before." He did not resist; flattered by her attention, they chit chat for awhile.

"Are you hungry? I'm a great Italian cook and live nearby. Interested?" asked Rose.

It was a one-night stand, but two months later, Al received a call from a panicked voice. "Do you remember me? I'm Rose. You came to my apartment, and I cooked an Italian dinner?"

"What are you saying? We had sex once! Are you sure?" Al asked in disbelief.

"Yes. I haven't been with anyone else since I met you and will not consider an abortion. I'm Catholic; it's against my religion. Can we meet to discuss this?"

"Yes. Let's meet in the lobby of the Hilton, Sunday at 2:00."

Rose did not expect to see an entire family sitting in the hotel lobby. After introductions Al said, "My parents are very concerned. They will offer you a substantial amount of money to reconsider an abortion. I'm still paying off student loans."

"This is your grandchild!" Rose declared as she looked at his mother and father.

No reasoning could change Rose's mind. They agreed to a small wedding in church. Al told his parents that he would have a quick divorce from this woman but pay child support.

Years later, when Gina became a teenager, her mother told her of the arranged marriage but added, "I was never sure it was your father." Rose became pregnant again and again. Al accepted to stay married for the children.

Returning home after my last visit with Al and his children, I now had some doubts about merging our families and being accepted as a step-mom. Plans for the move to Olean were scheduled for the end of June after school closing. As usual I had too many clothes to pack; I seldom discarded old clothes, style usually returns.

It was early afternoon, a Monday, when the phone rang and I slowly reached to answer.

"Dad is dead." The cold voice speaking was Gina. No preparation for this horrible news. "Will you be coming for the funeral? Arrangements haven't been made yet – too soon."

I screamed, feeling as if someone had plunged a knife through my chest. "No, no, it's not true, are you sure, Gina? When did it happen?!"

Completely shaken I didn't think I could continue this conversation. Gina continued, speaking quickly, wanting to end this call, "He was playing tennis and collapsed on the court. A neighbor called an ambulance, but it was old, and when they tried to revive him, the equipment backfired, and he died instantly."

"This is too much. I can't think. Too painful–will have to call you back," I said.

Julie heard my screams and rushed upstairs to see me shaking uncontrollably, tears covering my face.

"Al is dead...life means nothing now. I cannot live without him. I have to be with him. I want to die! This is too painful!"

"If you die, I DIE, TOO!" said Julie. "Don't you love me?" She held me tight.

I have experienced death many times before, my father, my sister, my one-day-old brother, grandparents...but Al's death touched me so deeply. Every fiber of my body was shaken. I truly wanted to die. Al, if you only knew how much I want to be with you, I thought. It's hard for children to understand the deep physical love between a man and a woman. I hope in their lifetime they will experience such a love.

I stared at Julie. Her words were like a cold shower over me. How can I expect a child to accept death? My death, it would be too cruel. I have to stay alive.

I reached out to her. "We love each other so much," I said through tears. "I promise to be there for you forever."

The phone rang again. It was Eric, Al's brother. We had never met, but I knew the brothers were very fond of each other.

"I find it hard to believe this news! I am also in shock," Eric continued. "Can you fly to Buffalo? I'm at his apartment now and will handle all the funeral arrangements since my mother is eighty and not well. She will fly in from Texas tomorrow. I will wear a name badge on my lapel and meet you at the airport. Let me know the time of your arrival. You can stay at this condo; I see many personal things here belonging to you. Gina is already here."

Buffalo, New York

Arriving at the airport the next day, it did not take long to find Eric in the crowd. He looked a lot like Al; they could have been twins. We held each other, still shaking.

"Thank you for the great happiness you brought to my brother's life. He often spoke of you and how much you loved each other."

We drove mostly in silence to the Buffalo condo, not far from the airport. Gina opened the door and offered no words of sympathy. My head was still spinning, recalling happy moments here. I sat quietly on the brown couch.

"You can have whatever you want...he has a great collection of guns. Interested?" asked Eric in an awkward voice, trying to make to feel better.

"No, just his large photo and recorder on the desk; I would like to hear his voice again."

"I don't see a recorder anywhere," Eric said.

Gina turned away from us with a mirthless smile.

"We should stop for dinner at a restaurant and then go to Olean. There is more room for us to stay there. I'll wash the few dishes in the sink," said Gina. Reaching for the detergent under the sink, she quickly pulled a small box with red letters, "rat poison," and as she gathered a few garbage items, she stuffed it in the bag and threw everything in the hallway chute. "Let's go now." Gina almost ran to the red convertible. "You can drive, Eric."

The distance between Buffalo and Olean was short, but the silence was unbearable. Eric tried desperately to make small talk; no one answered.

Staying at the house was hard, remembering my last visit. Sara and Al's mother greeted me affectionately. Gina left to be with her mother a few doors away.

Eric agreed to attend to all the funeral arrangements; a brief Lutheran service at the funeral parlor would be scheduled for the same day with an open casket. I approached the casket, still hoping to see someone else...no, it was definitely Al. I kissed him on his lips, my tears covering his face, touched his hand, not ready to let him go.

Sara was standing next to me, and reaching out, started unbuttoning her father's shirt.

Horrified, I asked with a chocked voice, "What are you doing?!"

"I want to see if an autopsy was performed. I think my sister Gina poisoned dad with rat poison; I saw the box she bought last week. She said it was needed at his apartment."

Eric, appalled, rushed to the casket and pulled Sara away.

It was all too much for me. I needed to be alone. I walked outside for some much-needed air. My chest was burning with pain, and I wanted to scream, "NOT FAIR!" But the words would not come out.

Rose did not enter the funeral parlor, but standing outside the building, I could hear her conversation with a friend.

"I sold the house to my attorney this morning. It's all legal. Margo gets nothing."

Don't Care

Whatever she did, whatever she does, nothing matters now.

Eric, the children, his mother, and myself stayed until the closing of the funeral home at 9 P.M. We all returned to the house in silence. I went directly to bed and did not wake up until early morning. Sara had prepared breakfast, but I could not eat.

The last visit to the funeral parlor, before closing of the casket, was painful. I kissed him again. A white hearse would carry his body. Sara and I asked to ride with him to this final journey to the cemetery.

To see someone you love so much being lowered in the ground is so emotional, I had to turn my head away.

GOODBYE, LOVE....
Published in Society of Poems 1976 by Margo Tarr.

Do you know Death?...She's a bitch! Offer your soul, plead, cry, scream, your cemeteries are overcrowded, why hoard bodies? She remains untouched, without mercy, she prostitutes it all and give nothing back, nothing! Where are you, Pandora and Hope?

Help me breath life in his beautiful body. I want to crawl in this casket and resurrect my love. As Hermod pleaded for Balder. Hela, I beg of you give him back to me…I love him so! Dressed in white and black ribbons today, I'm bride and widow. A hearse instead of a limousine we ride the final journey together. I cannot live in the hell…he was my life. No one hears my cries!

Gina was standing very close to me. She pulled my arm and said, "I need to talk to you, let's go by the Buick." The minister was still praying over Al's grave, but obviously Gina was in a rush.

Gina, still pressing on my arm, said, "Dad had promised me this car for my eighteenth birthday next week."

"Your father told me that he had already transferred the title to my name for use of the Buick when I live here," I answered.

"Even if I wanted to give it to, I don't know where the title is."

Gina quickly opened the trunk, where it appeared my luggage had already been placed. How did it get there from the house? Strange…Al was meticulous about documents, title in the trunk?

Gina reached for a tan envelope. "I have it. You just need to sign the title…here…I have a pen and the extra keys."

DON'T CARE. I signed.

"I can drive you to the airport, nothing at the house for you to return to there. Eric and his kids can drive back with Al's good friend Joe," said Gina.

Eric, his mother, and children hugged me and said goodbye. Gina drove me to the airport in the Buick, speeding anxious to be relived of my presence, plowing through traffic lanes. She dropped me off at the first boarding terminal, though mine was Delta at the end, quite a walk.

Minutes later, a short distance away, a terrible sound could be heard like an explosion. Flames bursting in the air…people gathered, trying to walk toward the scene. I stopped almost frozen. An airport security guard tried to hold the crowd from running toward the scene.

"Stay back, it's too dangerous. Looks like a speeding car, red convertible, going the wrong way crashed with a semi. Doubt anything can be done. Everyone, you need to board on with your flight."

Should I wait? Prolong this stay if it is Gina? My children at home need me. I have to get home and get over this nightmare.

Fairness is what justice really is.

It was all too much for my delicate constitution, crying constantly, waking up in the middle of the night, feeling Al's arms around me, wanting to vomit, nothing there. I felt that I was on the verge of a nervous breakdown.

My sister Louise called a few weeks later, listening to me she became afraid that my situation could worsen and offered us, my children and I, to share her home and family temporarily. I accepted. She lived in Ottawa, Canada, my favorite city, and hopefully, emotionally, I would eventually be able to make decisions regarding our lives and where to live. Louise truly saved my life.

Week later I contacted companies and scheduled interviews. I was offered a position in Ottawa City Hall, great pay, and being Canada's capital made it all the more interesting and political.

My children were not excited at the prospect of moving to a different country, different school system, and making new friends.

"Mom, even their mail boxes are a different color," cried Willy.

I did not accept the job.

Return to Florida

All my dreams and hopes had disappeared. There was a void in my heart that I tried to heal outwardly but knew would never heal inwardly.

I needed to return home to make plans for my children and myself; time was precious.

My ex-husband and I had agreed that our daughters, Carrie and Julie, would move to my condo in Daytona Beach and our son would remain with him in Cincinnati. He had continued to pay child support and alimony through this whole ordeal, making life financially bearable, and for that I respected him.

The trip was exhausting. I was not used to driving long distances. We stopped twice at motels along the way. Almost there in Daytona, I noticed a large posted sign on the front door of an adjoining hotel to the Towers: HELP WANTED.

"Carrie, hurry up and write down that number! I need a job and want to call."

We quickly unpacked, had a McDonald's dinner, and the girls changed into their bathing suits to make a dash to the pool.

The Palms is a beautiful hotel, walking distance to the Towers. I decided not to make a phone call appointment but to apply in person since I usually made a good impression.

I entered the large marble floor lobby with huge chandeliers and large beige leather chairs. In a corner sat an elderly man at a Louis XIV highly carved desk. Very impressive!

"I am Aaron Well, owner. Can I help you?" he asked.

"I saw your poster and just moved here, in need of a job," I responded.

"Sit. Do you have a resume?"

"Yes, but it's not updated. I would like to know something about the position."

He looked very briefly at my resumé and said, "Secretary, receptionist, social events, thirty-five hours a week, the pay is low. Interested?"

I could do all those jobs, and with child support, I could make it.

"We have a small staff. Jobs are scarce in Florida, everyone wants to live here, my waiter/bartender has a master's degree and couldn't get another job anywhere here. I managed to save this hotel from bankruptcy last month with the help of labor union bosses. There are a few permanent residents, few tourists; we can barely cover expenses."

Thinking fast...there were benefits to working in walking distance from the condo. How often does one walk to work with sand in their shoes?

"I accept. When can I start?"

"Tomorrow. My wife will explain the small switchboard. There are not too many reservations, two permanent residents, living on their trust funds, a ninety-year-old attorney John Ogilvie and his eccentric wife Carol."

The girls were on spring break from school, and it was easy enough for them to leave the condo, and there was a twenty-four-hour security guard and receptionist who screened all visitors coming in.

There were a few interesting incidents at "The Palms." One evening I received a call from Mr. Wells, the owner. He was concerned with his permanent resident, Attorney Ogilvie, since his wife had not returned after one of her special trips by taxi ten miles away to her favorite McDonald's for a special burger she claimed she couldn't get anywhere else.

"We need to prepare a tray of food for Mr. Ogilvie. He has not eaten all day. My waiter Bob will go with you to his room and please stay to see that he eats."

Bob and I took the elevator to the penthouse. Knocking on the door, I said, "Mr. Wells sent you a tray of food. You are probably hungry."

A 6'4" tall thin man, completely naked, answered the door.

"My wife is not here. I don't think it would be appropriate for you to come in."

Bob slowly pushed the door open and found a robe on the bed to help Mr Ogilvie cover his naked body, no belt. Desperately looking Bob found panty hose on the floor and used it to keep the robe closed.

It was very embarrassing to sit opposite this very formal attorney, trying to make conversation. He ate most of the food. Carol, his wife, returned an hour later.

Two other events happened at The Palms a few months later, again with Carol Ogilvie.

While at the switchboard, I received an unusual call from the minister of the local Episcopal Church.

"A florist has just delivered a large bouquet of flowers for the wedding of Carol Ogilvie and Frank Sinatra. I have nothing in our books to perform such a wedding. Do you have a resident by that name?"

I replied, "Yes, she resides here but has personal problems. Cancel the wedding request, we will get back with you, and thank you for calling."

Aaron Wells, hotel owner, had a long conversation with Carol. She denied it all. His last episode with the Ogilvies was much more serious. Carol did not like the politics of the current Florida Governor and had made several threatening calls to his office about his view recently aired on the news.

That morning the news promoted a rally by the Governor just a few miles away, and everyone was welcome. Carol reached for her gun from the bedside nightstand and called a taxi.

Carol came running out of the front door lobby where a taxi cab was waiting and screamed out, "I'm going to a rally, do not tell my husband!"

Shortly after her departure, two tall men dressed in tan overcoats, like a TV action scene, came in the hotel looking around.

Seeing no one but me, one man flashed a badge and said, "FBI looking for Mrs. Ogilvie, the Governor has received a serious call from this hotel."

"She left not long ago, probably going to the rally," I said.

Without another word, the agents rushed out the doors. Carol was almost there, but the taxi was delayed by the long lines to hear the speaker. Agents having driven well over the speed limit parked the car and ran on foot to the cab. Opening the door, they retrieved the gun, handcuffed her, and led Carol on the long walk back to their car.

Carol Ogilvie was directly sent to a psychiatric ward of the general hospital, and John Ogilvie was placed in an assisted living facility. After sixty years of marriage, they were apart for the first time.

I enjoyed my late afternoon walk from the office with sand in my shoes, hurrying to the condo to make a large pitcher of lemonade for my girls, and for myself, a tasty vodka martini with three olives. We all sat on the very long balcony facing the ocean, making small talk. Life was good again.

The holiday season was almost upon us. My daughter Carrie had kept in touch with her many friends in Cincinnati, especially a former boyfriend who was urging her to return. He wanted to marry her; she was fifteen-years-old.

"We need to be with dad and Willy for Thanksgiving! Can we move back? I have no friends here," cried Carrie.

I accepted; wrong decision. I believe that we are solely responsible for our choices and have to accept the consequences, sad.

Months later I contacted William to help with the move back. In November the weather in Cincinnati is miserable, icy roads and snow. Why was I leaving sunny Florida, the sound of the ocean rocking me to sleep...for my children?

THANKSGIVING

My condo in Daytona Beach sold a few months later for $30,000. Two years later, it was on the market for $300,000. Real estate like the stock market has its up and downs, but this was unprecedented. I missed the ocean and the last memories with Al there. It was a magical year of travels and love.

For Thanksgiving I prepared the usual feast: turkey, cranberries, sweet potatoes, green beans, and gravy. We all sat at the table, except William, who remained standing and looking serious.

I wondered if he was going to say a prayer. Was that possible? He was slobbering his words since he had already poured a third gin in his coffee and then said, "I want a divorce."

Not surprised at his behavior but feeling hurt for our children, as they bowed their heads in silence, I replied, "I agree, but let's discuss this tomorrow. Tonight let's eat turkey."

Where to restart my life again and financially survive?

THE KENTUCKY SIDE OF THE OHIO RIVER

HISTORIC TOWNHOUSES FOR SALE 223 & 225 E 2ND STREET

I contacted a former real estate friend, Harriet Burns, President of the Northern Kentucky Association. We had cooperated on several projects with Kentucky and the Cincinnati Board of Realtors.

"You should get a real estate license, you already know the industry," she said. "Thomas Moore College is offering courses in preparation for the licensing, and you should move to Northern Kentucky."

It wasn't easy going back to school, but remembering my mother's words of wisdom, "You're all you've got. The power is in your hands." I decided to move forward. That decision effected the quality of my life for years to come.

Later my daughter Carrie joined the Church of Scientology, married and divorced. My son joined the Navy and toured the world. My daughter Julie became a scholar with two Masters degrees in mathematics and a PhD in math education.

LAND LADY

Covington, Kentucky was very familiar to me. I had several close friends living along the Ohio River on Second Street, which was lined with 100-year-old buildings.

A recent real estate sign posted on a six-family brick 100-year-old building was on the market for $105,000. Excited about the possibility of owning an income producing property, I made an offer for $95,000...ACCEPTED!

I contacted my son, who was still in the Navy at sea to be a co-owner. Interest rates were very low in the 1980s, and with income from the remaining tenants, we were able to obtain a mortgage with a closing date less than thirty days away.

The city of Covington was situated in a highly walkable area to Cincinnati. It was founded in 1815 when a trio of men, calling themselves the "Covington Company." purchased 150 acres on the west side of the Licking River that flowed into the Ohio River. The name was chosen in honor of their friend General Leonard Covington, an officer who died in the War of 1812.

It was almost impossible to sleep, counting the days to my move and being a land-lady. Late the night after closing, I received a call from the fire department informing me that my name was listed as the owner of the building on Second Street, now on fire. In a state of shock, I quickly dressed and drove with great speed to Covington. Neighbors were standing in the street, flames and smoke billowed from the top floor. I rushed to find the Fire Marshall for an explanation. The current tenant, a captain on a tour boat on the Ohio River, was known for smoking pot, and apparently a lit cigarette had landed on the floor and caused the fire. The captain was nowhere to be seen, and he never did return. His cat did not survive the fire.

Although a licensed Realtor, I had never been a land-lady. I soon realized how much I needed to learn about qualifying and screening tenants. Being a sympathetic soul, I listened too often to their sob stories for not being able to pay the security deposit and/or poor references.

Enough! Enough!

My delicate soul could not take anymore. I decided to sell the six-family building on Second Street. We would have made a great profit, except for the fact that the IRS considered it commercial property, which resulted in a small profit due to incompetent accountant. Thus ended my multi-family investment – forever!

Fifteen years later, that six-family building was purchased by a local developer and converted to a two-family, completely restored, and went on the market for $475,000. I purchased a condo nearby at "Governor's Point," with a federal-style architecture, bordering the Licking River with brick-paved, gas-lit streets, just minutes from downtown Cincinnati. I loved life at Governor's Point and spent several years in my beautiful condo with a flower garden facing the main street. I was very active in the community there. It felt like home.

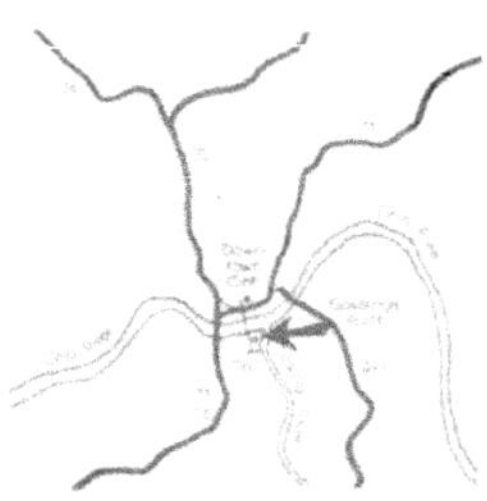

Look at life in Cincinnati a whole new way.

323 East Second Street • Covington, Kentucky 41011 •

Sister Cities International

The Sister Cities concept originated in early post-World War II days when town affiliations between the U.S. and other countries began. This concept became official in 1956 when President Eisenhower proposed the People to People Program, which in 1967 evolved through the National League of Cities' assistance into the tax-exempt non-profit Town Affiliation Association of the U.S., Inc., which principally contains Sister Cities International (SCI), with the headquarters in Alexandria, Virginia.

The purposes were to meet the challenges of improving international relations, to deepen human understanding, and to promote world peace through personal diplomacy and the exchange of technology and cultures.

The most influential event was the establishment of a Sister City with Cincinnati, Ohio and Gifu, Japan.

The city needed a Public Relations person for this committee to promote its activities. I was the PR Director for a major commercial real estate company, so somehow my name was submitted to become the PR Director for Sister Cities...

With the help of Dr. Henry Morozumi, Chairman of Cincinnati-Japan Society, businessman, scientist, and the first Japanese citizen to go to the North Pole, we included an extensive network of volunteers and the mayor's assistant to develop a relationship between the two cities. We procured a TV newscaster and a photographer.

In 1995 we sent 181 Cincinnatians to our sister cities and received 357 people from our sister cities. These people participated in exchanges of all kinds: business, educational, and cultural. Many of our sister city visitors stayed with local host families. Cincinnatians, too, often stayed with local families during their sister city visit.

With the help of Doctor Henry Morozumi.

Our first objective was to raise money to pay for the trip to Gifu, Japan for Cincinnati Mayor, the Chamber of Commerce and Northern Kentucky University representatives. Companies, such as General Electric (GE), Proctor & Gamble (P & G) and Cinergy, were very generous with their financial contributions.

We all flew on Japan Airlines. The service was impeccable; stewardesses dressed in dark pantsuits, wearing white gloves, served a very delicious steak dinner, including tea and orange juice. Hot napkins for our hands followed. We had been advised to walk around the plane frequently because of the long eighteen-hour flight by way of Alaska to Tokyo. Looking out my window, seeing northern snow peaks, I felt as if I had left the planet. Other than a few air pockets, the trip was smooth sailing.

What an arrival in Tokyo! We were greeted at the airport by two Gifu State Senators, the Mayor, and translators. A large delegation was holding signs, "Welcome to Japan." We breezed through customs thanks to Dr.

Morozumi. Japan Airlines had printed cards in Japanese and English to help in communicating during our one-week visit.

The airport is very much like many others, except here very few westerners, a term often used in Japan, including "western bathroom."

Our destination, Gifu, is located on the Niagara River, mid-way between Tokyo and Kyoto. With a history stretching back 1,000 years, Gifu was the site of many famous Japanese battles.

We boarded a chartered bus to the Okino Hotel, which boasts a very impressive lobby. We were greeted by half the hotel staff, helping with a ridiculous amount of luggage service.

Tale out service is what the Japanese deliver best.

I was surprised to see several Japanese men chatting in the lobby, wearing only kimonos, a custom for changing out of business attire to a more relaxing style of dress after the day's work. Most Japanese men are short and have soft voices. It's almost relaxing, like saying, "I want to share my thoughts with you." I wanted to learn Japanese.

At the hotel, my room was all decorated in pink, the bed with satin sheets was covered with a rose duvet and French provincial furniture. We only had a half hour to get dressed to meet back with our delegations at the hotel coffee shop; not a coffee shop by our standards. It was very elegant with all male servers.

The only two girls in this Cincinnati group were myself and Stella, who had just returned from business trips to three other countries, very tired, just wanting to sleep and rest.

We could hear an animated discussion by a few of the younger guys where to find a Gisha house; obviously they were in the mood.

Dr. Morozumi had planned an elaborate schedule for meeting with the Mayor of Gifu, his staff, several company executives, and school children.

Channel 5 newscaster and photographer were more interested in filming the city and its people.

Anxious to start our visit, Dr. Morozumi gathered us to go over the agenda. Our first tour was to visit the American Embassy, where we only met his PR attaché and staff. We were disappointed in its façade, surrounded by a tall wrought iron fence with the U.S. symbol and address. Next on the agenda, a meeting with Japan's Minister for External Trade Organization (JETRO), an exclusive and very expensive membership; its purpose to advise the government on the economy and promoting small investors in the U.S. Joining is a must if interested in doing business with Japan.

The Boardroom was very impressive; heavily carved long table, stuffed arm chairs all around, and a huge flower arrangement in the center. The main speaker was the former Ambassador from Japan to Washington, very articulate in English. Orange juice and coffee, in cups, are always served at such meetings by Japanese women wearing white gloves.

Another meeting on the agenda was with the Minister of Trade. Our delegation was all seated on one side, and Japanese counterparts with similar business titles were facing us. Did we all forget the purpose of meeting to establish a Sister City, I wondered.

Tired from all these meetings, I still wanted to join our group to go "out on the town." Our host for the evening recommended MAHARATAJA disco, very upbeat and expensive, especially expensive was the liquor! Waiters were all males in dark uniforms. I was assigned a young boy, not a geisha, next to me on his knees, ready to refill my champagne glass or whatever I needed. I have to admit, it was a warm feeling to be so pampered!

Young Japanese girls, in their twenties, save money for one month to pay $50 for the entrance fee to this club in hopes of meeting a financially successful, young potential husband.

We were all invited to the Senator's home; their families had lived there for 500 years. We sat on a cushion on the floor with our legs crossed and were entertained by several Japanese women dressed in the traditional style, using umbrellas while singing and dancing. It was quite enjoyable.

The formal signage of documents by the cities of Gifu and Cincinnati were attended by hundreds of Japanese citizens, officials, and the media, lots of cameras. The honorable mayor Makiga gave an eloquent speech with the words, "We are now married."

Cincinnati Mayor Luken, speechless, jokingly replied, "I hope my wife doesn't hear about this!"

Japanese Wedding Reception

Cormorant Fishing

Our last evening in Gifu, we were driven to the Nagara River to board a special boat to view and experience the fishing by Cormorant Fishermen, a title passed on by father to son. It takes ten years to become a cormorant fishing masters.

Cormorant fishing on the Nagar River is a 1,300-year-old tradition where fishing masters use Japanese cormorants to catch fish, primarily aya (Sweetfish). Because of the great skills of the fishing masters, they have received the official title of "Cormorant fishermen of the Imperial Household Agency."

When the cormorants catch the fish, they are brought back to the boat using ropes attached to their bodies. When they are back in the boat, the fishing masters remove the fish from the birds' throats. Each bird can hold up to six fish in its throat. The birds are prevented from swallowing the fish because of a ring tied around its neck. The cormorants, however, are still able to swallow smaller fish. Thought the ropes are strong, the fishing masters are able to quickly break them if a bird's rope gets caught beneath rocks, ensuring the bird will not drown.

Follow guide with red flag...don't get lost !

Each night cormorant fishing officially begins when three fireworks are set off in the evening sky. At first the boats come down the river, one by one, catching fish. They use a fire attached to the front of the boat to attract the fish and hit the sides of the boat to keep the birds active. As the night draws to a close, the six boats will line up side-by-side and descend the river in a process called sougarami.

In addition to the cormorant boats and the viewing boats, other boats play a role in the evening. The first boat to provide entertainment for the evening is the dancing boat (odoribune). There are usually five dancers on the boat while it goes up and down the river, entertaining the visitors before the night's cormorant fishing begins. Additionally a refreshments boat follows each of the boats on the river, giving visitors a chance to buy snacks, drinks, and fireworks to use before cormorant fishing begins.

Ending the evening, we were to view an exceptional display of fireworks, including six-foot tall red letters of Cincinnati firework along the river. Spectacular!

The next day, early morning, we boarded the "Bullet" train, SHINKANSEN. A type of passenger train which operates on Japan's high-speed railway network at an incredible speed. Its lavatory is a hole in the floor. One must squat very low...quite an exertion on the body. You only have minutes to disembark from the speeding train, throw your luggage out first, and jump on the platform on your way out! An experience not to be forgotten.

We must have seemed like strange creatures to the Orientals we met as we differ so much in appearance. Stella was a 5'6" blonde, me with red hair, which was often touched and pulled by young Japanese women as a sign of good luck.

We all returned from Japan well and happy to be back in Cincinnati, truly a memorable and unique experience!

Everyday Japanese Expressions

Hello
kon-nee-chee-wa
konnichi wa

Good morning
o-ha-yaw-goz-eye-mass
ohayō gozaimasu

Good afternoon
Good day
kon-nee-chee-wa
konnichi wa

Good evening
kom-ban-wa
komban wa

Good night
o-vass-oo-mee nass-eye
oyasumi nasai

Good-bye
sye-aw-narra
sayōnara

See you later
ja matta
ja mata

Yes
high
hai

Please
on-eg-eye shee-mass
onegai shimasu

Yes, please
high on-eg-eye shee-mass
hai onegai shimasu

Great!
ee-dess nair
ii desu ne

Thank you
arry-gattaw goz-eye-mass
arigatō gozaimasu

Thank you very much
daw-maw arry-gattaw
goz-eye-mass
dōmo arigatō gozaimasu

That's right
saw dess nair
sō desu ne

No
ee-ay
iie

No, thank you
ee-ay kek-kaw dess
iie kekkō desu

I disagree
wattash-ee wa saw
om-oy-mass-en
watashi wa sō omoimasen

Excuse me/
Sorry
soo-mee-mass-en
sumimasen

Don't mention it/
That's OK
daw ee-rash-ee mash-tay
dō itashimashite

That's good/
I like it
ee dess nair
ii desu ne

That's no good/
I don't like it
yok-oo nye dess nair
yoku nai desu ne

I know
wakkattem-ass
wakatte imasu

I don't know
shee-ree-mass-en
shirimasen

It doesn't matter
kam-eye-mass-en
kamaimasen

Where's the toilet, please?
toy-ray wa dokko dess ka
toire wa doko desu ka

How much is that? (point)
sorray wa ee-koorra dess ka
sore wa ikura desu ka

Is the service included?
sah-beess-ree-aw ga
height-tem-ass ka
sābisu ryō ga haitte imasu ka

Do you speak English?
ay-gaw ga dek-ee-mass ka
eigo ga dekimasu ka

I'm sorry…
soo-mee-mass-en ga…
sumimasen ga…

I don't speak Japanese
nee-hon-go ga hanass-em-ass-en
nihongo ga hanasemasen

I speak only a little
Japanese
nee-hon-go ga skosh-ee shka
hanass-em-ass-en
nihongo ga sukoshi shika
hanasemasen

I don't understand
wakka-ree-mass-en
wakarimasen

Please can you…
…koo-dass-eye
…kudasai

repeat that?
koo-ree-kye shtay
kurikaeshite

speak more slowly?
mot-taw yook-oo-ree hanash-tay
motto yukkuri hanashite

write it down?
kye-tay
kaite

What is this called in
Japanese (point)
korray wa nee-hon-goddair
nan-toh ee-mass ka
kore wa nihongo de nan
to iimasu ka

Marge Schott
and the Cincinnati Reds

Marge Schott, Cincinnati Reds President, was very active with the Gifu, Japan-Cincinnati Sister City Project. She hosted several events for the Gifu and Cincinnati committees at her fifteen-acre estate in the village of Indian Hill. In the very spacious home, every room detailed an era long past, incredible fireplaces in nearly every room secret door and passages. The Cincinnati committee, when invited, not only attended but included their spouses. She never objected to large crowds.

When in town, Gifu representatives often attended the Reds baseball games. Marge Schott always sat in the front row with a red phone in hand and her Saint Bernard dog "Schottzie" by her side. One deplorable incident happened at a baseball game with some of the attending senators from Japan. Suddenly popcorn was being thrown at the Japanese representatives by some "seniors" a few rows behind. Embarrassed I rushed directly to their seats to interfere.

"We fought against the Japs in the last war!" one man shouted.

"I believe the war is over," I replied and returned to my seat. End of popcorn war.

Margaret Unnewehr-Schott died at the age of seventy-five and donated $1 million to St. Ursula Academy and $1 million to the Dan Beard Boy Scout Troop for an 18.5-acre lakeside camp.

8505 Blome Rd

Sister Cities' Ambassador's Ball

A fundraiser and silent auction was held at the Cincinnati Art Museum to benefit the seven Sister Cities of Greater Cincinnati.

- Liuzhou, China
- Gifu, Japan
- Munich, Germany
- Kharkiv, Ukraine
- Harae, Zimbabwe
- Nancy, France
- Taipei-Hsien, Taiwan

Special guests included Amos B. Muvengwa Midzi, Ambassador of Zimbabwe, Terumi Muramatsu, Counsel of Japan, Dr. Richard Schade, Counsel of the Federal Republic of Germany, and Cincinnati Mayor Roxanne Qualls.

The most original performance was with drums; the traditional songs and dances by the "Thunderbirds," a tribal group traveling throughout New York State demonstrating their cultural heritage. Their colorful costumes, feathers and leather, were spectacular. Our foreigners were totally impressed.

It was a financial success with almost 200 in attendance. The money was distributed among the seven cities. Months of work, great cooperation with many volunteers, I was proud to be its chairperson.

Now ninety years young, I'm still on a committee. GFWC - General Federated Woman's Club of Clearwater, founded in 1890, is a non-profit organization whose members donate their time, talents, and financial resources to serve the community. I co-chaired several fashion shows with GFWC, my past years at the John Robert Powers Modeling School were a great help with these events.

Growing old should take longer; the memories are fading slowly, plaques on my walls, brief fame, so few years left. I cannot stop the aging process. Should I end it all while I'm still in control? If tomorrow is the end of my life and today was my last day, couldn't I say I've had enough pains and struggles?

NOT YET! Adieu tristesse, bonjour joies.

"Courage is not having the strength to go on but going on when you don't have the strength." (Teddy Roosevelt)

Event Chairwoman Mrs. Margo Tarr-Boyington with the Honorable Japanese Consul, Mr. Terumt Muramatsu, the Honorary Consul of Germany, Dr. Richard Schade and His Excellency Ambassador of Zimbabwe, Africa, Amos B.M. Midzi